IN THE LINCOLN COUNTRY

Journeys to the Lincoln Shrines
of Kentucky, Indiana, Illinois
and Other States

BY

REXFORD NEWCOMB

PROFESSOR IN THE UNIVERSITY OF ILLINOIS, MEMBER OF THE
AMERICAN HISTORICAL ASSOCIATION, KENTUCKY STATE
HISTORICAL SOCIETY, ILLINOIS STATE HISTORICAL
SOCIETY, INDIANA LINCOLN UNION, ETC., ETC.

WITH 43 ILLUSTRATIONS AND SKETCHES
AND 8 MAPS

PHILADELPHIA & LONDON
J. B. LIPPINCOTT COMPANY
1928

TO THE MEMORY OF
THEODORE LINCOLN BERGEN
THE FATHER OF MY WIFE AND
A DIRECT DESCENDANT OF THE
LINCOLNS OF OLD HINGHAM
THIS BOOK IS DEDICATED

FOREWORD

THIS book is in no sense to be taken as a biography
of Mr. Lincoln. The writing of the life of our
first martyred president must be entrusted to other
hands. Indeed many splendid minds have already
essayed this task and even the most superficial Lincoln
admirer is familiar with a number of excellent studies
of this nature. My task is a far humbler one: the
making of a book that will give accurate and adequate
information regarding those hallowed spots in Kentucky, Indiana, Illinois, and other states made memorable by Lincoln's life or presence there.

Today, thousands yearly make pilgrimages to the
Lincoln shrines. Last year, (1927), in excess of 134,000
men, women, and children from every state in the
Union and many foreign lands made the trip to Springfield, Illinois, and signed the register at the Lincoln
Monument. The number increases each year and this
is true at other Lincoln memorials throughout the
country.

In order to aid these countless thousands readily
to prepare themselves for such visits and make it
possible for them to have adequate, authentic, and
practical information upon the many spots of interest
connected with Mr. Lincoln's life, this book of "little
journeys" to the various Lincoln shrines has been
written. The author has made many visits to the
places named in years gone by, but, in order to bring
all facts about them up-to-date and to give the latest
information regarding the roads leading thither, he
has, during the preparation of this volume, again gone
over the whole territory with camera in hand and
note-pad handy. Detailed maps of each of the im-

7

portant sections of "The Lincoln Country" are included, and these may be followed much as one uses the popular automobile maps. It is hoped that this volume will make a long looked-for pilgrimage to the spots hallowed by his footsteps possible and easy for many an admirer of "the greatest American."

The writer is under obligation to the staffs of the Kentucky State Historical Society at Frankfort and of the Illinois State Historical Society at Springfield, for various helps and aid, to Mrs. Mary Webber of Urbana, Illinois, for permission to reproduce an hitherto unpublished letter of Mr. Lincoln, to the curators of the various Lincoln shrines for co-operation in the accomplishment of his purpose, to Judge Lawrence B. Stringer of the Logan County Court for data on Lincoln, Illinois, to the Studebaker Corporation for a photograph of the Lincoln carriage, to Professor T. E. O'Donnell of Urbana for a photograph of the old Vandalia Capitol, to Caufield and Shook, photographers of Louisville, Kentucky, for permission to use their copyrighted photographs, and lastly to the large body of Lincoln admirers who have helped with suggestions and encouragement.

REXFORD NEWCOMB

Urbana, Illinois
Lincoln Day, 1928

CONTENTS

ILLUSTRATIONS

Illustrations

MAPS

THE TRAVELS OF THE
EARLY LINCOLNS

THE OHIO AT ROCKPORT, INDIANA

CHAPTER I

THE TRAVELS OF THE EARLY LINCOLNS

THE line that brought forth Abraham Lincoln had its American beginnings in Massachusetts about 1637 when on June 20 of that year Samuel Lincoln, born in England around 1619*, arrived in the port of Boston. In England, Samuel had been apprenticed to a weaver, by name Francis Lawes, and we may picture the lad going about his work at the loom, running errands for his master, or performing menial tasks for his master's family. It was a hard life the apprentice had in that day in England, for as yet those "reforms" which afforded better conditions for labor had not come about.

But Samuel was not long to remain in his native land, for in 1637 Francis Lawes decided to come to America and Samuel, under the rule of the craft guild to which he was apprenticed, was considered a member of the master's family. Thus he came to America with Lawes and went with him to Salem. Samuel remained at Salem for only a brief period, however, for soon he removed to Hingham, across Boston Bay to the south, where others of his name had preceded him.

The Lincolns are a numerous people in Massachusetts and New England, and Mr. Charles Z. Lincoln estimates that Massachusetts alone contributed 335 soldiers of that name to the Revolutionary army,

---

* Some say as late as 1619, upon August 24 of which year a Samuel Lincoln was baptised at Hingham, County Norfolk, England. Whether this Samuel Lincoln was the lad who arrived in New England in 1637 is still unsettled, but upon the assumption that the Lincolns of Hingham *New* England were the descendants of Lincolns of Hingham *Old* England, a bust of President Lincoln has been set up in the old church in the English town.

15

among them Major-General Benjamin Lincoln. At the time of the Revolution, however, few of the name lived outside of New England, for the same authority finds only six Lincolns in the Continental Army from places outside this area.

The first two generations of the Abraham Lincoln progenitors remained in Hingham, the third generation removing to New Jersey and then to Pennsylvania, the fourth to Virginia and the fifth, Abraham Lincoln's grandfather, to Kentucky. Below is set forth the paternal line of the President as given by Mr. Waldo Lincoln* of Worcester, Massachusetts, Doctor W. E. Barton, and other students of Lincoln's ancestry.

I—SAMUEL LINCOLN

Born in England about 1619. Died at Hingham, Massachusetts, May 26, 1690. His wife, Martha, died at Hingham, April 10, 1693.

II—MORDECAI LINCOLN

Son of *Samuel* and *Martha Lincoln;* born at Hingham, Massachusetts, June 14, 1657. Married for the first time about 1685 to Sarah, daughter of Abraham and Sarah (Whitman) Jones of Hull, and for the second time to Mrs. Mary (Hobart) Chapin, February 17, 1702. He died at Scituate, Massachusetts, November 28, 1727.

III—MORDECAI LINCOLN

Son of *Mordecai* and *Sarah Lincoln;* born at Hingham, Massachusetts, April 24, 1686. He removed to Freehold, New Jersey, where he married Hannah Salter, daughter of Richard Salter of that place. He married a second time Mary Robeson of Amity township, Berks County, Pennsylvania, probably about 1729, and died in Amity, May 12, 1736.

IV—JOHN LINCOLN

Son of *Mordecai* and *Hannah Lincoln;* born at Freehold, New Jersey, May 3, 1716. He married a Mrs. Rebecca

* *History of the Lincoln Family.*

(Flowers) Morris in Pennsylvania, July 5, 1743, and in 1773 removed to Linville Creek, Rockingham County, Virginia, where he died in 1788.

V—ABRAHAM LINCOLN

Son of *John* and *Rebecca Lincoln;* born in Berks County, Pennsylvania, May 13, 1744. He removed to Rockingham (then Augusta) County, Virginia, and in 1770 married Bathsheba Herring. He removed to Kentucky in 1782 and was killed by Indians on Floyds' Fork, Jefferson County, in May, 1786.

VI—THOMAS LINCOLN

Son of *Abraham* and *Bathsheba Lincoln;* born on Linville Creek, Rockingham County, Virginia, January 6, 1778. At the age of four he was brought to Kentucky. He married *first* Nancy Hanks, June 12, 1806, and *second* Mrs. Sarah Bush Johnston, December 2, 1819. He died in Coles County, Illinois, January 17, 1851.

VII—ABRAHAM LINCOLN

Son of *Thomas* and *Nancy Lincoln;* born February 12, 1809, on Nolin Creek, Hardin (now Larue) County, Kentucky. He married Mary Todd of Lexington, Kentucky, at Springfield, Illinois, November 4, 1842. He died at Washington, D. C., April 15, 1865.

Not long after Samuel Lincoln settled in Hingham, Robert Peck, the pastor of the church at old Hingham in England, and Daniel Cushing, arrived in the New World. Settling at Hingham, both became influential in the community. Cushing became a merchant in the new town and acted as town clerk. It is to his careful record of what transpired in the town that we owe much of our knowledge of the comings and goings and the daily life of these stern-faced Puritan people. Indeed it is in Cushing's account book that a notice of Samuel Lincoln's death is recorded, thus: "26 Monday old Sam Linkoln dyed of the small pox."

Samuel was apparently a God-fearing Christian man for he lived and died in the church, and church membership was a stern business in those days. He

was an industrious young man, for we soon hear of
him as a property owner. He purchased five acres of
ground in Hingham and here he brought his wife,
Martha, probably about 1649. This good pair raised
a numerous family, eight of their eleven children living
to ripe old age. The family attended Old Ship Meet-
ing-house in Hingham, built in 1681 and still standing,
and upon his death in 1690, Samuel was laid to rest
in the old burying ground, long since destroyed by an
unmindful populace.

Four sons and four daughters survived Samuel
Lincoln and the third of these sons was Mordecai,
from whom the line that gave the world Abraham
Lincoln was to descend. To the eldest son of the
family, Samuel, the old homestead was bequeathed at
the father's death, and to Daniel, the second son, fell
the task of cultivating the land that the family owned.
Mordecai, therefore, had to find a livelihood outside
the family circle. He was the second son of this name
in the family, a baby boy two years older having borne
the name for but three short weeks. This second
Mordecai was of firmer clay, however, and grew up to
be a strong, self-reliant lad. His physique, moreover,
was enhanced by the trade which he selected for a life
work—blacksmithing—and good health permitted him
to round out a vigorous three score and ten years. He
went across the bay to Hull to learn this trade, and
here he fell in love with and married Sally Jones.

Mordecai and Sally Lincoln lived in Hull for many
years, and here doubtless were born their first two
children, Mordecai, Jr. and Abraham, the first of that
name in the Lincoln family, christened, presumably,
for his grandfather Jones. Eventually, however,
Mordecai moved his family to the newly established
town of Cohasset, near Hingham, and here on Bound
Brook in 1691 he built a mill dam and set up a water-
power sawmill to furnish timbers for a developing
community. Once the sawmill was in operation,

Mordecai went upstream a short distance and here built another dam to run a gristmill that he established at this point. Not satisfied with two mills, he again built a third dam at a point above the second and here he erected a power forge and eventually a furnace, thereby becoming one of the earliest producers of iron in America.

Water made cheap power and Mordecai Lincoln prospered. Once the furnace was in operation and good iron was available, his forges and power hammers were busy turning out the many articles of iron needed in a growing community. With mills making lumber, grinding grain, and producing iron articles, he multiplied his wealth, leaving at his death what was considered a large estate at that time.

Some ten years after the removal to Cohasset, Sarah Lincoln died, and early in 1702 Mordecai married Mrs. Mary (Hobart) Chapin, a widow of Braintree, for whom he built the fine old colonial house near the mouth of the brook upon which stood his mills. This house still stands today, one of the most pleasant old houses within the limits of the town of Scituate. Here Mordecai died November 28, 1727, and they laid him to rest in Groveland Cemetery where his grave and that of his second wife are easily identifiable to this day.

Long before Mordecai's death, Mordecai Jr. and Abraham had left the parental roof, and, like many New Englanders of their day, they found their way to New Jersey, then recently wrested from the Dutch by England and a country heralded far and wide as a land of promise. They betook themselves to Freehold, where they operated a forge, and shortly Mordecai married Hannah Salter, daughter of a large landholder of the vicinity. Both Mordecai and Abraham acquired land here and Mordecai held land in New Jersey up until the time of his death. They were not long to remain in New Jersey, however, for there seemed a better opportunity for iron working in Pennsylvania. Mordecai entered into a company that built an iron furnace and forge on the Schuylkill River above Philadelphia, but in 1725 he disposed of his interest, investing the sale money in Berks County (Pennsylvania) lands, and in acquiring new holdings in New Jersey. Meanwhile Hannah, his wife, had died, and in 1729 he married Mary Robeson, probably the daughter of an Andrew Robeson who lived in Amity township in Berks County. In 1730 Mordecai acquired a new tract of 300 acres and here three years later he built the comfortable old Dutch type farmhouse still standing. He died here on May 12, 1736.

By Hannah, Mordecai had five children, who survived their mother, and Mary bore him three, the last of whom, an Abraham, was born after his father's death. When he died Mordecai gave his New Jersey lands to Hannah's children, leaving the Berks County lands to Mary's children. The oldest of Hannah's children was a boy, John, born at Freehold, May 13, 1716. It was to John that Mordecai looked to improve the estate that he had left in New Jersey, but John, like many of the Lincoln family before and after him, had eyes upon a new frontier and instead of returning to New Jersey after his father's death, he remained in Pennsylvania, marrying there Mrs. Rebecca (Flowers) Morris, a widow with one child.

In those days, there was a movement of people from the older parts of Pennsylvania into the newer parts of that state, and especially into the fertile valleys of Maryland and Virginia. The road that ran southward into the Virginia country passed through Berks and Lancaster counties and eventually John and his family were to obey the prevalent impulse and take that road southward to new opportunity in a new land. John had prospered in Pennsylvania, doubtless learning much of thrift from the Quakers, Dunkards, and Amish settlers who lived near him in the Schuyl-

kill Valley. We do not know what impelled him to
leave Pennsylvania, but presumably it was the promise
of cheaper lands and an opportunity to make money
in the newer country. Perhaps he wanted to afford
his grown and growing sons the advantages of getting
established in a new country. At any rate, in 1768 he
purchased a tract of 600 acres on Linville Creek in
what is now Rockingham County. Linville is a tributary of the Shenandoah River, and is situated in one
of the most beautiful valleys in all Virginia.

John and Rebecca Lincoln had nine children,
among them one, Abraham, the grandfather of the
President. John was a man fifty-two years of age
when he purchased land in Virginia, and later removing thither, he lived here until his death in November,
1788. Abraham was born when his father was twenty-
eight, and was thus twenty-four when his father
acquired land in Virginia. When twenty-six he married
Bathsheba Herring of Virginia, said to have belonged
to one of the aristocratic families of the section, and
three years later he was given a tract of about two
hundred acres, a portion of his father's original purchase on Linville Creek. To this he later added fifty
acres by purchase.

Abraham was a robust man and took part in the
local militia, holding a captaincy. That he was well
respected we may believe for from 1776–78 he served
as judge advocate of the court. Like his father and
grandfather, however, he longed for a new land, and
as early as 1780 made a trip to Kentucky. Here, in
May of that year, he entered 400 acres of land on
Floyd's Creek in the eastern part of the present Jefferson County and about fifteen miles from Louisville,
and on June 7 following he entered 800 acres more
which were situated further south on Green River.
Both these tracts were "entered" on Treasury Warrants.

At this time Kentucky was a portion of Virginia
but the same year that Abraham Lincoln entered

these lands, old "Kentucky County, Virginia," was divided into three counties of which Jefferson was one. The others were Fayette, named for General LaFayette, and Lincoln, named in honor of Major-General Benjamin Lincoln of the Revolutionary Army. Kentucky was not to be admitted as a state until 1792, or ten years after the Virginia Lincolns became identified with the fortunes of this new west.

For a good many years before Abraham Lincoln had decided to remove to Kentucky, that great transmontane area had been prominent in the minds and hopes of the people of the middle Atlantic states. A speculative mania began as early as 1737, but it was not until 1749 that the government of Virginia granted to Bernard Moore a tract of land at the mouth of the Ohio. From 1737 until the Revolution this "mania for speculation in western lands . . . developed, with ever accelerating force; each year greater and greater became the westward push; . . until . . . there was hardly a prominent man in Virginia who was not taking a flyer in western lands."*

Many colonies were projected in this territory. One was organized by Pennsylvanians to be known as Vandalia. Another known as the Transylvania Company was organized by North Carolinians. This company, which succeeded in buying lands from the Indians, was the enterprise with which Daniel Boone associated. Boone was in the employ of Richard Henderson, the moving spirit of this scheme when he made his first tour of western Kentucky. Under Henderson's directions Boone marked the "Wilderness Trail," which was the best land route to Kentucky.

With glowing accounts of Kentucky constantly in the air, and with many old friends and neighbors moving westward into this new land, it is not strange that Abraham Lincoln should have turned his eyes

* Alvord, C. W. "The Daniel Boone Myth," Jour. Ill. State Hist. Soc. XIX, 25.

westward. His original trip to Kentucky in 1780 was
followed two years later by the removal of his family
to the west. Thus with his wife, Bathsheba, and four
children, Abraham left the Linville Creek farm for
Jefferson County, traversing the old Wilderness Road
through the Cumberland Gap.

The family with others moved along the trail until
they reached the land that Abraham had filed upon,
and here the first Lincoln settlement in Kentucky
began. The farm was situated on Long Run, a tributary of Floyd's Creek, near the present line between
Jefferson and Shelby counties. In fact it is not improbable that the Lincoln cabin was one of a group
then known as Hughes' Station.

It was necessary for the colonists to remain close
together because of the hostility of the Indians, for in
August of the very year that the Lincolns arrived in
the country, Bryan's Station in Fayette County was
surrounded in the night by 600 hostile Indians led
by the notorious renegade, Simon Girty.

These were days in the new country that called
for heroism and fortitude on the part of women as
well as men, and one had always to be prepared for an
emergency. But things went well for Abraham Lincoln
for several years, and up until the time of his death,
he continued to acquire property in Kentucky. But
life in the new country was at best not to be long for
Abraham, and in May, 1786, while working in his
clearing near Hughes' Station, an Indian in ambush
shot from the woods, striking him down. His three
sons, then mere lads, were with him at the time.
Mordecai, the elder, hastily sending Josiah to the fort
for help, "ran into the cabin, and, pushing his rifle
through a crack between the logs, prepared for defense.
Presently an Indian came stealing up to the father's
body . . . Mordecai took deliberate aim . . . and
brought him to the ground." This revenge was of
little satisfaction, however, for his father was dead.

This left Bathsheba with five children; Mordecai a lad of fourteen, Josiah twelve, Thomas, the father of the President, eight, Mary and Nancy.

The location of the father's grave is unknown, but Dr. Barton believes that it lies within the enclosure of the Long Run Baptist Church which, built in 1797, stands today upon a portion of the land pre-empted by Abraham Lincoln.

Bathsheba remained in Long Run until the autumn of 1786, at which time she removed with her children to Washington County (formed in 1792 but at the time a part of Nelson County), where the father of the future President grew to manhood. Her removal thither was probably influenced by the fact that in that section lived Captain Hananiah Lincoln, a cousin of her husband, who had come to Kentucky with their party. He was a landowner of some importance and had been appointed to a captaincy in the militia. To Washington, Bathsheba took her little flock and settled near friends and relatives not far from the site of the future Springfield (founded 1793), the present capital of the county. Bathsheba appears on the tax rolls as late as 1794, at which time Thomas was sixteen, but apparently Mordecai had assumed charge of the land, as it was assessed to him.

How long Bathsheba kept her family together we do not know. We do know, however, that she was still living in Washington and maintaining a home as late as 1797, and that in 1801 she signed for the approaching marriage of her daughter Nancy. At this latter date she was presumably residing at the home of her son, Mordecai. She spent her declining years at the home of this daughter, who married William Brumfield, on Mill Creek in Hardin County. She died in 1836 and is buried in the old Mill Creek Cemetery.

There is some evidence that Thomas Lincoln made a trip to Tennessee somewhere around 1797 or 8. He went there to visit an uncle, Isaac Lincoln, who had gone from Virginia to the Watauga Valley of eastern Tennessee. How long he remained with his relatives is not quite plain, but he was back in Washington County by 1799, appearing on the tax list of that year. He probably returned to the farm of his brother, Mordecai, on Beach Fork, where no doubt his mother was then living. But he was not long to remain here, for his own career called for a removal elsewhere.

IN THE LINCOLN COUNTRY
OF KENTUCKY

CHAPTER II

THE MARRIAGE PLACE OF LINCOLN'S PARENTS

THE movements of young Thomas Lincoln are not always plain, but we are sure that he was not "a wandering laboring boy," as he has often been pictured and as his distinguished son once said. He doubtless helped for a time upon the farms of his brothers Mordecai and Josiah, the latter of whom purchased land adjacent to that of Mordecai in Washington County. Thomas saw his brothers established in homes of their own and he too looked forward to the time when he should have land and a home. Perhaps already he had thoughts of marrying and settling down as his brothers had done.

Just how long he remained on Beech Fork we do not know, but the time could not have amounted to much more than a year. At any rate by 1800, apparently, he had apprenticed himself to Joseph Hanks, a carpenter of Elizabethtown, the new county seat of Hardin, which county had been partitioned from Nelson County in the same year (1792) that Washington County had been constituted. Hardin was the county in which he was to spend his early married days and in which his illustrious son was to be born.

As early as 1783 Abraham Lincoln, Thomas' father, had acquired land in what was later to be Hardin County. This land was situated on Green River and was doubtless purchased as an investment, for he never settled upon it. Thomas himself was to acquire land in Hardin County, purchasing his first place as early as 1803 and paying for it with money presumably received in settlement of his father's estate. This farm which contained 238 acres, is situated on Mill Creek,

a branch of Salt River, about twelve miles north of
Elizabethtown on the old Shepherdsville road, and not
far from Mill Creek Church where his mother lies
buried. It is about six miles east of the present Dixie
Highway at a point about ten miles north of Elizabethtown (see map).

Thomas came to live upon the tract but it is difficult to say how long he remained as he was as yet unmarried. He retained title to the place until the fall
of 1814, at which time he sold the tract to Charles
Melton, whose descendants still own and live upon a
part of the original property.

Not far away from this farm lived Thomas Lincoln's two sisters: Mary, who married Ralph Crume,
and Nancy, who married William Brumfield. Perhaps
the removal of his sisters to the neighborhood accounts
for his purchase of land here. One wonders why, in
view of the fact that he was as yet unmarried, his
mother did not come to make a home for him. She
could not have been much over fifty-five years of age
at the time. He appears, however, to have kept
"bachelor's hall" on the place, but the probability is
that he was actually little there, spending most of his
time at carpentering in Elizabethtown and other villages of Hardin and adjacent counties.

In the course of the next three years he must have
been back on Beech Fork several times, casting longing
eyes at the winsome lass, who, as Miss Tarbell thinks,
lived with the Berrys, adjoining Mordecai's farm. But
just who was this girl? That is a question that has
caused the ablest students of the Lincoln history a
great deal of trouble. Dr. William Barton, speaking
at Springfield in 1924 said: "The paternal line of
Lincoln's ancestry is . . . well established, but his
maternal line is in worse confusion than it was twenty-
five years ago. Meager at best was the material for an
accurate history of the Hanks family. They kept no
records. They duplicated names in constantly over-

STEPHENS COLLEGE.
COLUMBIA, MO.

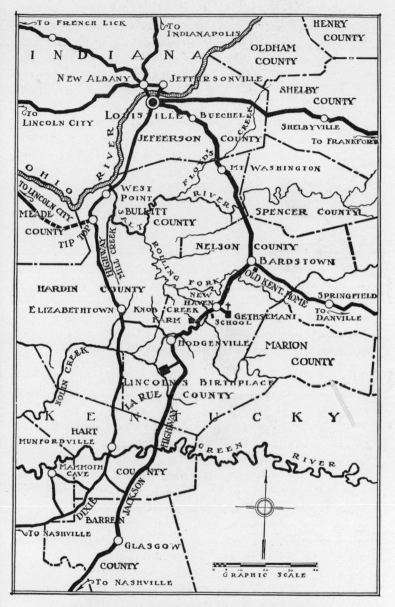

MAP OF THE LINCOLN COUNTRY OF KENTUCKY

lapping generations. They were highly migratory. It was difficult to find a basis for a consistent account of their wanderings and domestic relationships."

I shall not go into all the ramifications of this question which has puzzled students of Lincoln ever since the President's death, but set forth simply what seems to me to be the truth in the light of the most recent discoveries made by students particularly interested in this phase of Mr. Lincoln's history.

At the Library of the University of Chicago is a manuscript from the hand of Dennis Hanks, who lived with the Sparrow family and who came to Illinois with the Lincolns in 1830. He spent the remainder of his life in Illinois, dying at Paris, Edgar County, October 21, 1892. From him, William F. Herndon, Mr. Lincoln's law-partner and biographer, drew a great many utterances which he utilized in drawing his conclusions about the mother of the President. Dennis Hanks knew the facts about the paternity of the President's mother, and when the biographies of Mr. Lincoln were being prepared, he gallantly prevaricated to shield a woman member of his family. The resulting conflicting statements have naturally led to no end of trouble for biographers of Mr. Lincoln.

The manuscript above referred to reads as follows:

"Dennis F. Hanks was born in Hardin County on the tributary branch of the South Fork of Nolin on the old Richard Creal farm in the old peach orchard in a Log Cabin 3 miles from HoginsVille. Thence we moved to Mercer County and staid there a Bout 3 years and moved Back again to the Same place and then Remained untill we moved to Spencer County, Indiana, this was I think in the year 1816 if my memory serves me Rite. My mother and Abe's mother's mother were sisters. My mother's name was Nancy Hanks. Abe's grandmother was Lucy Hanks, which was my mother's sister. The woman that raised me was Elizabeth Sparrow, the sister of Lucy and Nancy. The other sister hir name was polly Friend. So you see there was 4 sisters that was Hankses."

This deposition throws some light upon the relationship of Dennis Hanks and Mr. Lincoln; that is Dennis Hanks was a cousin of Nancy Hanks, the wife of Thomas Lincoln and the mother of the President.

In 1899 Mrs. Caroline Hanks Hitchcock, of Cambridge, Massachusetts, published a small volume entitled "Nancy Hanks: The Story of Abraham Lincoln's Mother," which, while it made some very curious genealogical and historical assertions, set forth a document of importance which its author had unearthed in her search for data that would prove her thesis. This document was the will of one Joseph Hanks of Nelson County, Kentucky, which was dated January 9, 1793 and probated the following May 14. In this instrument the said Joseph Hanks names his wife "Nannie" (Ann), to whom he left a life use of his property, and eight children as follows: *sons;* Thomas, William, Joshua, Charles, and Joseph; *daughters;* Elizabeth, Polly, and Nancy. To Joseph he bequeathed his farm of 150 acres; to each son he gave a horse and to each daughter a "Heifer Yearling." No doubt before this time land settlement had been made upon the other boys as was then and still is the custom.

But Dennis Hanks says that Nancy was his mother and that her sister Lucy was "Abe's mother's mother." No Lucy appears in the will of Joseph Hanks and therefore a number of students of the problem have claimed that there was never any such person, the testimony of Dennis Hanks and the Hanks tradition to the contrary notwithstanding. What then became of this Lucy Hanks and, if living, why was she *not* mentioned in the will of Joseph Hanks? Rev. William Barton concludes that "Nancy Hanks, the mother of the president . . . was the innocent reason why her mother Lucy" was *not* mentioned in the will of her father and why she "did not receive a heifer."

"But," continues Dr. Barton,* "was the moral

* Trans. Ill. State Hist. Soc., 1924, p. 131.

standard of the Hanks family so high that Joseph
Hanks cherished his wrath nine years after the birth of
his little granddaughter and cut off his daughter Lucy
without a penny for no other reason than that one
youthful indiscretion? No; the moral standard of the
Hanks family was not so high as that, and *no family's
standard ought to be of that sort;* * but unfortunately we
know all too well that Joseph Hanks had later and
very strong provocation,† and that his disinheritance
of Lucy was no inadvertance. Lucy had caused him
great sorrow, both in Virginia and in Kentucky. At
the time of her father's death she was married and
living a respectable life, but he died without granting
her forgiveness."

Herndon ("Abraham Lincoln," 1896 Edition, Vol.
I, 3) carries this story. "On the subject of his ancestry
and origin I only remember one time when Mr. Lincoln
ever referred to it. It was about 1850, when he and
I were driving in his one-horse buggy to the court in
Menard County, Illinois. . . . During the ride he
spoke for the first time in my hearing of his mother,
dwelling on her characteristics, and mentioning or
enumerating what qualities he had inherited from her.
He said, among other things, that she was the daughter
of Lucy Hanks and a well-bred but obscure Virginia
farmer or planter; and he argued that from this last
source came his power of analysis, his logic, his mental
activity, his ambition, and all the qualities that distinguished him from the other members and descendants of the Hanks family." Thus it would seem that
Mr. Lincoln himself (if correctly quoted) was conversant with the name of his grandmother and understood the circumstances surrounding his mother's
birth.

Nancy Hanks was born in what is now Mineral
County, West Virginia, in 1784, and was brought to
Kentucky the same year when Joseph Hanks and his

* The italics are mine.   † See Barton, "A Life of Abraham Lincoln," I, 59

family removed thither. When the little Nancy was
seven years old, her mother married Henry Sparrow of
Mercer County (April 3, 1791). Henry Sparrow and
John Daniel "swore out" the license necessary for the
marriage of Henry to Lucy Hanks. Lucy had no
guardian but John Daniel swore "that she was of age"
and under the attest of Robert Mitchell and John
Berry, she executed the following document:

I do sertify that I am of age, and give my approbation
freely for Henry Sparrow to git out Lisons this day or enny
other day. Given under my hand this day, Apriel 26th,
1790.

Lucey Hanks.

They were married nearly a year later by Rev.
John Bailey, a Baptist minister, living long and
honestly and raising a large family, amongst them two
ministers. Many of the descendants of Henry and
"Lucey" live to this day in the "cut-off" of Anderson
County, Kentucky, southwest of Lawrenceburg where
the village of Sparrow, the church once served by a
son of Lucy, and Sparrow Cemetery are to be found.
The road from Lawrenceburg to Bloomfield and
Bardstown leads through this country.

Elizabeth Hanks, Lucy's sister, also married a
Sparrow, Thomas Sparrow. Their marriage bond in
the Mercer County Court House in Harrodsburg is
dated October 17, 1796. Thomas and Elizabeth
Sparrow were splendid people. They had no children
of their own, and they gave a home to the unfortunate
Nancy Hanks and her cousin Dennis Hanks, the son
of Nancy, the sister of Elizabeth and Lucy, by Charles
Friend. This Charles Friend was a brother of Jesse
Friend who married the fourth sister, Polly Hanks,
and apparently he never assumed any responsibility
for this son, born out of wedlock. Dennis Hanks always
admitted that he was "base born," but he always
shrank from saying as much about Nancy Hanks
Lincoln.

These good people, Thomas and Elizabeth Sparrow, proved "real" parents to Nancy, and after Nancy's marriage to Thomas Lincoln, their families lived near each other in the Nolin Creek district, where Abraham Lincoln was born. In fact so much attached to Nancy were they that, when the Lincolns moved to Indiana, they followed them there, as indeed did Nancy Hanks Hall, the mother of Dennis Hanks, and her husband Levi Hall, whom she married after Dennis' birth.

In order to make plain the mixed relationship of these people, I present herewith a diagram of the family of Joseph Hanks, the facts for which are gleaned from the writings of Dr. Barton, Mrs. Hitchcock, Rev. Louis Warren, Miss Ida M. Tarbell, Herndon and others. (Page 36.)

It will be noted in the diagram that Joseph Hanks had a son Joseph who married Mary Young. This was the carpenter of Elizabethtown to whom Thomas Lincoln apprenticed himself. Thus we see that Thomas was apprenticed to the uncle of his future wife and indeed it is more than likely that he may have become acquainted with her through her uncle. Miss Tarbell and others make Nancy live at the Richard Berry farm in Washington County near Lincoln's brother Mordecai. Be that as it may, it is *certain* that Thomas Lincoln and Nancy Hanks were married on June 12, 1806, at Beechland, the home of Richard Berry.

The marriage bond of Thomas Lincoln is still extant and may be seen at Springfield, Kentucky, together with "the return" of Rev. Jesse Head the officiating minister. This bond to which Thomas Lincoln and Richard Berry set their hands for the "full sum of fifty pounds current money" had as its condition that "there is a marriage shortly intended between the above bound Thomas Lincoln and Nancy Hanks." Richard Berry sets himself down as guardian ("garden") and John H. Parrott signs as witness. The bond is dated June 10 but from the "return" of

JOSEPH HANKS (died 1793)
M. NANNIE (Ann)

Thomas	William	Joshua	Charles	Joseph Jr.	Elizabeth	Polly	Nancy	Lucy
	M. *Elizabeth Hall*			M. *Mary Young*	M. *Thomas Sparrow*	M. *Jesse Friend* brother of *Charles Friend.*	Mother of *Dennis Hanks* by *Charles Friend.*	Mother of *Nancy Hanks* by a Virginia planter.
	John Hanks William moved to Illinois, settling near Decatur. John, his son, split rails with Abe in Macon Co.			Was the carpenter of Elizabethtown with whom Thos. Lincoln learned his trade. Later removed to Illinois, settling near Quincy in Adams County.	Foster parents of Nancy Hanks Lincoln and Dennis Hanks.		Later married *Levi Hall.* Squire Hall a son of this marriage.	Married in 1791 *Henry Sparrow,* a brother of Thomas Sparrow.

the Rev. Mr. Head we learn that the marriage was
solemnized two days later. Mr. Head, a deacon in the
Methodist church, lived upon a small farm not far
from the Berrys.

Weddings in those days were gay and boisterous
affairs and were generally followed by an "infare," in
this case given by the Parrotts. Doctor Christopher
Columbus Graham, who was for many years associated with the medicinal springs at Harrodsburg, and
who, born in 1787, lived to be over a hundred years
old, in his old age believed that he had attended this
wedding. The "Doctor," whose portrait hangs in the
collections of the Kentucky State Historical Society
at Frankfort, and who could not have been more than
nineteen years of age at the time, claimed that he was
in the vicinity of Beechland gathering "roots" and,
hearing of the approaching wedding, went, "just to
get a good supper." He claimed also to have attended
the infare given by John H. Parrott whom *he* cites as
Nancy Hanks' "guardian."

"We had bear meat," says the Doctor, "venison,
wild turkey and ducks; eggs, wild and tame, so common
that you could buy them at two bits a bushel; maple
sugar, swung on a string, to bite off for coffee or
whiskey; syrup in big gourds, peach-and-honey; a
sheep that the two families (the Berrys and the Parrotts) barbecued whole over coals of wood burned in
a pit and covered with green boughs to keep the juice
in; and a race for the whiskey bottle."

This last mentioned event was in Kentucky known
as the "ride for Black Bettie." It was a rollicking
backwoods custom to ride for "Black Bettie" just
before the wedding ceremony. The game was for the
young men of the party to mount their horses, gallop
over a pre-arranged course to the goal, which consisted
of a bottle of the best whiskey. The first man to finish
the course claimed the bottle, drank, passed it from
rider to rider, who drank toasts to the bride and

groom, and then all proceeded to the scene of the ceremony.

The log cabin in which Thomas and Nancy Lincoln were married is still in existence, although alas, not upon its original site at Beechland in Washington County. A few years ago it was acquired by enterprising citizens of Harrodsburg, the oldest town in Kentucky, and was taken down and removed to a site in that city where it was erected in the park just in front of the historic burying ground of old Fort Harrod. Not far away there has just been erected a replica of the original Fort which had long since disappeared. An inscription on the house reads "Lincoln Cabin Rebuilt. In this cabin at Beechland Thomas Lincoln and Nancy Hanks, parents of Abraham Lincoln, were married by the Rev. Jesse Head, June 12, 1806."

The staunch old logs, carefully "dovetailed" at the corners, the rafters of sapling poles, the "sawed" (not "puncheon") floor, the batten door, the sturdy chimney and picturesque roof of split "shakes" are typical of the rugged pioneer architecture which so perfectly expressed the hardy life and rigorous ideals of that day. It is a "document" as important in its way as is the birthplace of Mr. Lincoln and should be as carefully preserved and safe-guarded.

A few squares away upon the broad slope of the hill-side lies the Harrodsburg cemetery and in that cemetery lies buried Jesse Head, the Methodist preacher who secured for himself a place in history by officiating at this simple backwoods wedding. Regarding this preacher, old Doctor Graham maintained he was no "old fogey" backwoods man. He was ahead of his time on many questions "and talked boldly against slavery, and Tom and Nancy Lincoln and Sarah Bush were just steeped full of Jesse Head's notions about the wrong of slavery and the rights of man, as explained by Thomas Jefferson and Thomas Paine."

MARRIAGE-PLACE OF LINCOLN'S PARENTS, HARRODSBURG, KENTUCKY

Miss Tarbell makes Jesse Head* a member of that branch of the Methodists who had separated from the main body of the church largely because of the differences of opinion upon slavery. Doctor Barton, in his "The Life of Abraham Lincoln,"† practically throws out of court Doctor Graham's testimony on this point by showing that Head was himself a slave owner until such time as his financial condition made it impossible for him to own slaves or for that matter much else of value. In fact his household goods were upon one occasion sold under the sheriff's hammer at the court house door in Harrodsburg, being "bid in" by George M. Head, the pastor's son.‡ General Robert McAfee credits Reverend Jesse Head with the discovery of the Harrodsburg Springs in 1806.§ He does not, however, mention this fact or refer to Jesse Head in his "Life and Times,"¶ although he gives considerable attention to the religion and preachers of his day. He tells us, however, that the "summer of 1806," when Lincoln's parents were married, "was extremely dry in the months of June and July," with "scarcely a shower of rain until the 28th of July, which saved the corn from total destruction. . . . In June there was nearly a total eclipse of the sun, and dust in the public road was several inches deep, the corn withered in the sun & much of the vegetation perished & many religious congregations held fast days."

In 1810 the Rev. Mr. Head moved from his farm near Mordecai Lincoln and the Berrys in Washington County to Harrodsburg, where he was to live for thirty-two years or until March 22, 1842, when he died. He was at first buried in his own dooryard, but was some years after the death of his wife in 1851

* Tarbell, "In the Footsteps of the Lincolns," 109.
† I, 18.
‡ Barton, "Life of Abraham Lincoln," I, 483.
§ Letter dated November 25, 1845, Draper Collection, University of Wisconsin.
¶ Register of the Kentucky State Historical Society, Vol. 25.

removed to the town cemetery. In 1922 the monument now seen above his grave was put in place.

Harrodsburg, which is one of the most interesting
and historic towns in Kentucky, is best approached
from Lexington, although a good highway is now (1928)
being built from Lawrenceburg. Leaving Lexington

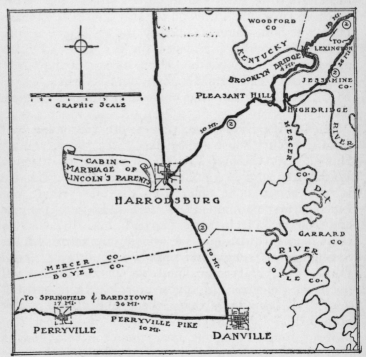

HARRODSBURG, KENTUCKY, AND ITS VICINITY

(via South Broadway) the Boone Way, an excellent
pavement, leads one by way of Brooklyn Bridge over
the Kentucky River (19 miles) where some very
picturesque scenery is to be encountered, through
Pleasant Hill, the old Shaker community, (4 miles) to
Harrodsburg (10 miles). Shakertown is itself very
interesting, with its quaint brick and stone houses, in
one of which is an excellent tourist hotel. Not far

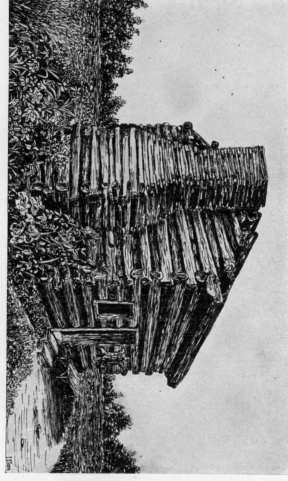

THE BIRTHPLACE OF ABRAHAM LINCOLN, NEAR HODGENVILLE, KENTUCKY

away is the famous Dix River Dam, a mammoth hydro-electric power development and near Shakertown is High Bridge over the Kentucky River.

One may approach Harrodsburg from Bardstown, coming via Springfield (Washington County) where the Thomas Lincoln-Nancy Hanks marriage documents are to be seen, and through Danville, one of the oldest towns in the state and the seat of Centre College. Here was born James G. Birney the abolitionist, once candidate for the presidency on the Liberty ticket and here lived Theodore O'Hara, author of the "Bivouac of the Dead" and Dr. Ephraim McDowell (1771–1830), the physician who made distinguished surgical history.

In leaving Bardstown, take Route 168, going east from the court house square past "My Old Kentucky Home" (See Chapter IV). This road leads through Washington and Boyle Counties. At Springfield one is only about eight miles from the place where the Lincolns first permanently settled and where Thomas and Nancy Lincoln were married, but the road to these spots (directions for which one must ask at Springfield) is rough and entails a fording of Beech Fork. The villagers at Poortown, on the creek, will point out the site of Mordecai Lincoln's cabin and tell you in all seriousness that "the President was really born here." Seventeen miles from Springfield one passes through Perryville, near which town was fought (October 8, 1862) one of the most deadly battles of the Civil War. In this engagement some 7,000 lives were lost. At Danville take Boone Way northward (10 miles) to Harrodsburg.

CHAPTER III

LINCOLN'S BIRTHPLACE

WHEN Thomas and Nancy were married they went to live in Hardin County, setting up housekeeping in Elizabethtown, the county seat and a village of some promise. Hardin was one of the older Kentucky counties, having been established by the first state legislature in 1792. Originally it was larger in extent than it now is, and from its territory six complete counties and parts of two others were eventually formed. Larue County, that portion of Hardin to which the Lincolns were soon to remove was, however, not cut off until 1843. Hardin County was settling up in these days and during the first decade of the nineteenth century its population doubled.

Thomas Lincoln evidently believed Elizabethtown a good place in which to settle, for here he had established his carpenter shop. While still a young community, Elizabethtown was by no means just a struggling outpost of civilization. The earliest settlers had been in the vicinity since 1780, at which time the Helms, the Hynes and the Haycrafts had settled, building three stockade forts within a mile of each other and upon the site of the present town. The second generation of the pioneer families were now prospering and this is evidenced by the fact that brick had begun to replace the cruder log houses of the village. Major Ben Helm had built a large brick house in 1803 and in December, 1806, the fine new brick court house was completed, giving the citizens of Elizabethtown considerable grounds for crowing over the inhabitants of the rival town on Nolin Creek, who sought the honor for their own place.

42

Moreover, Elizabethtown could boast of churches
—a Baptist society, the second in Kentucky, had been
established in 1781—schools, taught by Ichabod
Radley, John Pirtle and the Rev. Benjamin Ogden, a
Methodist minister, a mill operated by the Haycrafts,
a debating society and a dancing-master. In spite,
however, of these evidences of prosperity and progress,
the majority of the inhabitants still occupied the log
dwellings that lined the scrawling street which stretched
itself across the southern face of Muldrow's Hill, upon
which the town was built.

But these log houses were constantly being en-
larged and made more comfortable, and craftsmen
like Thomas Lincoln, James Perceful and Rev. Mr.
Ogden, himself "a good worker in wood," found ample
employment for their hands. And Lincoln had need
for work for in February, 1807, the first child, a
daughter Sarah, was born.

Tradition in Elizabethtown has it that Thomas
Lincoln built the cabin into which he moved with his
bride. The spot has been located upon what was then
apparently a plot of ground belonging to a Mr.
Houston. The site was only a few hundred feet north
of the point where the present Dixie Highway crosses
Mill Creek near the Louisville and Nashville Railway
Station. An old, leaning, poplar tree shades the spot
today. Rev. Louis Warren tells us that during the
residence of the Lincolns in Elizabethtown, Thomas
was engaged in the construction of a large sawmill for
Denton Geoghegan and that several of the houses
which he helped to build were still standing fifty
years ago.

But the pioneer urge was to get land, and Thomas
Lincoln, like other poor men, wanted a home and
broad acres like those of the Helms and Haycrafts,
and thus, when little Sarah was eighteen months old,
the Lincolns moved fourteen miles down the country
to Hodgen's Mill (now Hodgenville), near which place,

on the Big South Fork of Nolin Creek in that part of
Hardin that is today known as Larue County, Thomas
Lincoln purchased a small farm upon which stood a
good log cabin. Stopping, apparently to work for a
time near Hodgenville, by late autumn or early winter,*
Thomas Lincoln had settled his little family in the
cabin upon this farm, and here upon February 12th
next was born that lad who one day was to become the
most honored of all Americans.

The cabin was a humble one, but was by no means
the lean-to shelter that it has often been pictured.
Of this we may be sure, for there is a tradition in the
countryside that the Lincolns had a "cow and calf,
milk and butter, a good feather bed, homespun
coverlids," a "loom and wheel" and the other simple
accoutrements that made up the household equipment
of the day.

This part of Kentucky, which is only about fifty
miles from the Mammoth Cave by modern highway,
and considerably less as the crow flies, is one of the
most picturesque portions of the state. It lies just
beyond the outer edge of the "blue grass," Muldrow's
Hill forming the boundary between what may be
called the "hill country" and the "blue grass." One
making the trip from Louisville may take one of two
routes: The Dixie Highway (U. S. Highway No. 31)
through Saint Helen's, West Point (21 miles), and
Elizabethtown (27.5 miles), or the Jackson Highway
via "old Bardstown Road" through Buechel (8 miles),
Mount Washington (20 miles), Bardstown (19 miles),
and Hodgenville (27 miles). Whichever road is taken
down, the other should be taken in return, in this way
making a "loop" through the "Lincoln Country of
Kentucky."

If one wants to see the Mammoth Cave, this too is
easily accomplished while in the vicinity. The places
are all upon the Nashville-Louisville route and one

* The farm was purchased in December, 1808.

coming from the south should take the Dixie Highway through Bowling Green and Cave City to the cave and northward via Elizabethtown to Hodgenville (Junction of Dixie Highway and Elizabethtown-Hodgenville Road two miles south of Elizabethtown), or via Buffalo to Lincoln's Birthplace, Hodgenville and Bardstown. (This latter route was partially under reconstruction during the summer of 1927.) The

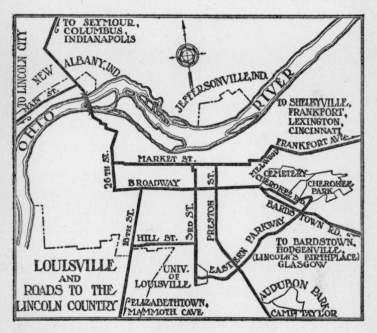

Dixie Highway crosses the Green River by toll-bridge at Munfordville.

Coming from Louisville via the Dixie Highway the first place of interest in the "Lincoln Country" is Elizabethtown. The visible record of the early Lincoln occupation of the town is scant, but places and documents connected with Sarah Bush Lincoln, the President's step-mother, and his father are to be seen. In the court house square there is a marker erected several

years ago which consists of a bronze tablet attached
to a stone secured from Thomas Lincoln's Mill Creek
farm (See page 29). It reads as follows:

> Thomas Lincoln and Nancy Hanks Lincoln,
> The Parents of
> Abraham Lincoln,
> Lived in Elizabethtown from the time of their marriage,
> June 12, 1806, until their removal in the fall of 1808, to the
> farm near Hodgenville where Abraham Lincoln was born.
> Sarah, their first child, was born here.
> A year after the death of Nancy Hanks Lincoln in Indi-
> ana, Thomas Lincoln returned and on December 2, 1819,
> married here Mrs. Sally Bush Johnston, a resident of Eliza-
> bethtown, who became the beloved foster mother of Abraham
> Lincoln.

A short distance north of the Court House on
Main Street and opposite the county jail, a tablet
upon a garage indicates the site of the home of Sarah
Bush Lincoln, removed several years ago, and at the
court house are several interesting Lincoln documents,
among them the appointment of Thomas Lincoln as
a "road surveyor" in 1816, and the marriage bond of
Thomas and Sarah Lincoln. The site of the Thomas
Lincoln cabin is pointed out near the "L. and N."
Depot.

Hodgenville is the next place of historic interest.
Here Robert Hodgen established his mill in 1788 and
the site of the mill is still to be seen within the limits
of the town (established 1818) at a point where the
dam crosses Nolin Creek. It is claimed that Lincoln
as a boy "went to mill" here. Not far away was the
Hodgen House which was for many years a well-known
tavern. Tradition has it that the French traveler
Michaux was entertained here in January, 1796, and
that the exiled Prince Louis Phillipe, later King of
France, stopped here in April, 1797.

In the public square of the town is Adolph Weinman's splendid statue of Abraham Lincoln erected

LINCOLN STATUE, HODGENVILLE, KENTUCKY
ADOLPH WEINMAN, SCULPTOR

from appropriations made by the State of Kentucky and the federal government, supplemented by private subscriptions. This excellent seated figure which was pronounced by the late Robert T. Lincoln to be a "noble" likeness of his father was unveiled May 31, 1909, upon which occasion Henry Watterson, the beloved Kentucky journalist, gave the principal address.

Two miles east of Hodgenville and just off the Jackson Highway, is an old stone house which, erected early in the nineteenth century, is reported to be one of the landmarks in the vicinity recalled by the President in later life. A mile and a half south of this house and a quarter of a mile off the road leading from the Jackson Highway to Leafdale Post Office is the site of Little Mount Church of which Thomas and Nancy Hanks Lincoln are supposed to have been members, and in its little graveyard Abraham Lincoln's little brother Thomas was buried.

Two and a half miles south of Hodgenville one comes to Nolin Creek. Along the gravelly pools of this little stream and among the wooded hills of this beautiful countryside the young Lincoln gained his first impressions of the great world of the out-of-doors. Here he picked wild flowers, chased the chickens and calf, listened to the call of wild things in the woods and wondered at it all. In the neighborhood lived the Enlows, the Brownfields and the Creals, but as yet, perhaps, the pleasant old cabin at the present entrance to the Lincoln Farm had not been built. At least it was not in its present-day, somewhat elaborate form. This was the Richard Creal homestead, and is generally dated about 1815, that is four years after Tom Lincoln had removed his family over "old Muldraugh" and up New Haven way.

The Lincoln cabin stood back a little distance from the road, upon a slight eminence and not far from a fine spring of water beneath the hill that is today fresh and clear. This, known as "Sinking Spring,"

was the source of water-supply for the Lincoln family.
Indeed the cabin which is said to have been built by
David Vance about 1805 owed its location to this
spring. Ample stone steps now replace the path that
Nancy Lincoln used to take in going for water.

To the Reverend Louis Warren, at one time pastor
of the Baptist churches at Elizabethtown and Hodgenville, we owe a knowledge of the documentary history
of the Lincoln Farm. He tells us* that the farm was
originally part of a 60,000 acre patent. "As early as
1786," says Mr. Warren, "John Dewhurst was in possession of one-half of this tract which he sold to William
Greenough the same year. By 1791, the 30,000 acres
was in the possession of William Weymouth and later
John Hood and Joseph James each purchased tracts of
15,000 acres. James disposed of his interests to
Richard Mather in 1798," and he it was, who, on May
1, 1805, sold 300 acres of this tract to the David
Vance above mentioned. Six months later Vance sold
the farm to Isaac Bush, who, on December 12, 1808,
sold the place to Thomas Lincoln for $200, cash.

Thomas Lincoln held possession of the place until
1813, when, according to Mr. Warren, "it was discovered there was a payment due Mather by Vance
that had never been settled. The property was thrown
into litigation and ordered to be sold, although Thomas
Lincoln was awarded the $200 cash which he had paid
for the land."

After passing from the hands of Thomas Lincoln
the farm was owned by various people and was further
subdivided until November 23, 1894, when the place
became the property of Alfred W. Dennette of New
York, a great admirer of Mr. Lincoln. Mr. Dennette
also acquired the old cabin, which in the 60's, had been
removed, and restored it to its original site.

The cabin thus restored to its old place by Sinking
Spring has had a romantic and varied history. After

* Abraham Lincoln's Birthplace.

the Civil War, George Rodman, an admirer of Mr. Lincoln, purchased it from Richard Creal, moving it to his farm about a mile and a half distant. Here it was first used as a negro cabin, but later as a tenant house. During 1872–3 it was used as a schoolhouse and when John Davenport married the school teacher in 1875, they went to housekeeping in it. They continued to occupy it until 1894, when Mr. Dennette purchased it and returned it to its original site.

Even then the cabin's travels were not over, for in 1897 the 143 logs of which it was composed were taken apart and shipped to the Nashville Centennial Exposition where it was displayed. After the fair it was removed to Central Park, New York, and in 1901 it was exhibited at the Buffalo Exposition. After this exposition the cabin was acquired by David Creer, who stored its substance in the basement of the old Poffenhausen Mansion on Long Island and from this dark retreat it was in 1906 resurrected by the Lincoln Farm Association. It was shown that year at Louisville and in 1909 was brought to Hodgenville preparatory to placing it in the Memorial on the Lincoln Farm.

The farm itself remained in Mr. Dennette's possession until he went into bankruptcy, at which time it was sold under the hammer at the Hodgenville Court House. This tract, which now composed less than one-third of the original Lincoln farm, was purchased on August 25, 1905, by the late Robert J. Collier, who, on November 9, 1907, presented it to the Lincoln Farm Association, an organization of contributors to a fund solicitated through *Collier's Weekly* for the purpose of erecting upon the farm a memorial in keeping with the sacred character of the spot.

The Association, founded in 1906, enrolled some 81,000 people, who raised $300,000 and on February 12, 1909, the one hundredth anniversary of the birth of Abraham Lincoln, the cornerstone of a memorial building to enshrine the cabin in which he was born was laid

by President Theodore Roosevelt. This splendid
temple, entirely enclosing the little cabin to protect it
from the elements and perpetually preserve it for
future generations, was erected at a cost of a quarter
million dollars, and, completed in 1911, was dedicated
on November 9 of that year by President Taft.

This beautiful structure, planned by the distinguished architect, Mr. John Russell Pope—who, by
the way, designed the much admired Scottish Rite
Temple in Washington, D. C., and many of America's
finest residences—is in every way appropriate to its
purpose and emblematic of the great soul of the man
whose birthplace it commemorates. Of staunch and
heroic proportions and executed in sombre granite, it
expresses in architectural form the character of the
rugged, upright, honest, serious Lincoln. Its gray
walls suggest a certain sadness that at times was so
characteristic of the man; its perfected form and delicate detail mirror perfectly the nobility and refinement
of his sensitive soul. There it stands atop a noble flight
of steps; a simple-cut block of granite—a flowering
out, as it were, of the very hills which surround it. Out
of these hills came Abraham Lincoln!

Just under the hill is Sinking Spring, one of the
prettiest spots of its kind I have ever seen, and not
far away is the "Corner Oak", as splendid an example
of this noble species as one would want to see. At a
point six feet above the ground its trunk has a circum-
ference of over fifteen feet, while its foliage in mid-
summer has a "spread of over one hundred feet."
Although known for its size and beauty as early as
1822, this tree seems perfectly preserved today. It
will doubtless last for many years to come. Old
surveyors from 1827 on used the tree as a landmark,
and it is said that today three land surveys make
this tree their starting point.

Sinking Spring Farm with so splendid a tree not
over three hundred feet from the house and others no

LINCOLN MEMORIAL, HODGENVILLE, KENTUCKY

JOHN RUSSELL POPE ARCHITECT

less fine in their way near by, and a water source like that under the hill, must have been a pleasant place, and although the young Lincoln removed to a new home when he was but two years old, we may picture the mother with little Abe and his sister spending long summer afternoons under the beneficient shade of this noble tree or, upon extra warm days, in the cool damp shade of Sinking Spring.

In 1916 the property was turned over to the United States, together with an endowment amounting to $48,000. Thus Lincoln National Park came into being. Since it was placed under the control of the War Department, the Secretary of War received it. President Wilson was present, however, and on September 4 made an address. Under the terms of gift to the United States "there shall never be any charge made or asked from the public for admission to said park or reservation," and every day of the year this shrine to the greatest of all Americans is open to the pilgrims who make their way to Sinking Spring Farm.

CHAPTER IV
LINCOLN'S KNOB CREEK HOME

WHEN little Abe was two years old his father had again decided to move, this time as before, not far away, but over "old Muldraugh" to its eastern side and therefore into a new valley. The road lay then as now over this famous hill, but that it was far more tortuous and less easy of ascent than at present one may well guess. It was this very road which traverses the country from Nolin to Bardstown of which Thomas Lincoln was in 1816 appointed a sectional surveyor or supervisor as we would now say. He superintended that portion of the road between the "Bigg hill and the Rolling Fork." The Rolling Fork is a branch of Salt River, and Knob Creek upon which the new home of the Lincolns was located flows into it.

Take the road from Lincoln's birthplace to Hodgenville (two and one-half miles), then six miles northeast over "old Muldraugh" and into Rolling Fork Valley. One and a quarter miles from the bridge on Jackson Highway at the foot of Muldraugh Hill and not far from New Haven is the Lincoln Knob Creek Farm. The spot is only about three miles from the place where Nancy first lived in Kentucky with her grandparents. It was here that the Lincolns were to live from 1811 until they removed to Indiana in the fall of 1816. The spot is unmarked except by a small sign placed there by the Louisville Automobile Club. The limestone hills, steep and wooded, form sheer boundaries for this pleasant little valley and from their sides the elements have scooped the rich soil that now makes the valley so fertile. It is a delightful place today with its oaks, sycamores and willows, and must have been a pleasant place when Lincoln lived here as a boy. This is the first home that he remembered, and years later as president he recalled several events connected with his life here.

Here it was that those sweet days of early comradeship with that delicate and sensitive mother, whom he was not to keep for many years, began. In later life he said of her, "My earliest recollection of my mother is sitting at her feet with my sister, drinking in the tales and legends that were read and related to us. All that I am or hope to be I owe to my angel mother." Thus he thought of his mother as any loving son must think of a mother who, in early and formative years, taught to him those sterling lessons of life and conduct that Nancy Hanks, the mother, taught to Abraham Lincoln.

From all we can learn of her she was a sensitive, sweet-souled, normal mother, dutiful to her husband, absorbed in her home, her family, the church and God. In his recent book* Doctor Barton gives us pretty but undoubtedly truthful pictures of the young mother, re-sings the songs she sang, reconstructs the day's work she did, shows with what pride she got out her best dishes and tried to make her best "corn pone" when the parson came their way. And she was the normal mother that plans and hopes and prays that *her* boy will one day "turn out" to be honest, upright, and true and "make his mark" in the world.

I think the world appreciates the contribution of this noble woman to the life of her illustrious son, but I am afraid that the motives of Thomas Lincoln are not always so well understood. His move of twelve miles over the hill has often been looked upon as the aimless wandering of a shiftless man. I do not believe that Thomas Lincoln was what could be called a provident man, but he wanted to do the best he could for his wife and little ones. He who goes over the

---

* "The Life of Abraham Lincoln," I, Chapter III.

road traversed by the family in moving from Sinking Spring Farm to the Knob Creek place will probably not be struck by the real motive that lay behind this move. Sinking Spring Farm with its rolling hills, its splendid spring, and its noble trees, all very lovely at almost any season of the year, will appeal to those who love the great out-of-doors. But Thomas Lincoln was concerned with very practical matters; he had to wrest a living out of these beautiful but none too fertile hillsides, and that was a difficult thing to do. So Tom Lincoln decided to move to a "better farm."

The site of the old cabin of the Knob Creek farm, long since demolished, is in a field on the left hand side of the road as one comes from Hodgenville, just beyond the point where the Jackson Highway crosses the Knob Creek bridge. Dr. Barton quotes Nicholas A. Rapier, who was born on the place, as saying that when he was a boy the house was used as a cattle shed by his father.* It was in the cabin that a third child was born to Thomas and Nancy, a second son named for his father. This child died in infancy and tradition has it that he was buried in the old cemetery at Little Mount Church.

It was at Knob Creek that Abe first went to school and the names of two of his early teachers, Zachariah Riney and Caleb Hazel, he remembered in later years. These early teachers were apparently near-by settlers who, capable of instructing the young by the old "blab-school" methods, taught a short term each year. Of his early schooling in Kentucky and Indiana, Mr. Lincoln afterwards said, "When I came of age I did not know much. Still, somehow, I could read, write, and cipher to the rule of three, but that was all." It was while attending this school, we are told, that Abe donned his first pair of trousers, changing to them from the long "tow shirt" which boys of the time wore.

* "Life of Abraham Lincoln," I, 79.

The old school was a log house about fifteen feet square with a broad-throated fireplace. It was about a mile and a half up the road from the Lincoln cabin and at the right just north of the present town of Athertonville. It stood upon a little elevation about three hundred feet from the road and within a hollow or gully. The building in ruined condition used to be pointed out some years ago, but was not in evidence during the summer of 1927 when I visited the place.

We know of Zachariah Riney that he was a Catholic. Many of this faith settled in this section of Kentucky and early the institutions of the Church began to develop here. Not far from New Haven is the Abbey of Our Lady of Gethsemani, founded in 1848 by the Order of Reformed Cistercians or Trappists. Austerity and piety in everyday life with perpetual silence is the daily practice of the monks of this order. Their picturesque church and monastic buildings and their well improved farms are quite worth the short detour that leads from the Jackson Highway (3½ miles) to their gate. James Lane Allen's beautiful story of "The White Cowl" has its setting at Gethsemani.

Bardstown, fourteen miles northward on the Jackson Highway, is a place of considerable historic and romantic interest, and as you journey thither glimpses are caught now and again of the picturesque Rolling Fork down which Thomas Lincoln was to push his boat on his first trip to Indiana. At Bardstown one sees the old Colonial Catholic Church, "the first cathedral west of the Alleghenies" with its marvelous collection of paintings attributed to Van Dyke, Van Bree, and Rubens, said to have been presented to the church by Louis Phillipe. In the public square of the town lies buried John Fitch, who preceded Robert Fulton in the invention of the steamboat and who for years lay buried in the quaint little cemetery in the rear of the century-old stone jail. Not far away is the old stone Talbot Tavern, still used, and a mile east-

ward of the court house is Federal Hill, the Judge
Rowan home, better known as My Old Kentucky
Home, where Stephen Foster wrote the song of that
name, "Massa's in de Cold, Cold Ground," and others
that have endeared the composer to all America. The
road back to Louisville is a gleaming highway through
a delightfully picturesque country. At a point about
two and six-tenths miles by the speedometer beyond
Mt. Washington, the highway crosses Floyd's Fork
of the Salt River. It was upon Long Run, a branch of
this stream, that the original Lincoln settlement in
Kentucky was made.

The Knob Creek farm was on the old Louisville-
Nashville road, one of the principal north and south
highways of the day, and men who knew the country
in both directions passed the Lincoln dooryard. Some
of these travelers stopped at the tavern kept by Caleb
Hazel's father and Tom Lincoln heard them tell of the
better opportunities for a poor man across the Ohio
in Indiana. Here land was easy to obtain and the soil
was said to be rich and the titles were from the United
States government, and thus secure. Indiana would
soon be admitted to the Union and such recognition
was bound to benefit the country.

Lincoln was having difficulty in getting a clear
title to the farm upon which he was living and so he
decided to make a trip to Indiana to look over the
country and, if advisable, select a home in that new
land.

Thus minded, in the autumn of 1816 Thomas constructed a flatboat on Rolling Fork near the mouth of
Knob Creek. The Jackson Highway today passes
the spot, a short distance below the bridge over the
Rolling Fork. Tom had had some knowledge of the
construction of flatboats, having made a trip to New
Orleans for Isaac Bush, a relative of the woman who
was later to be his wife. Completing the craft he

secured four hundred gallons of the best local whiskey and loaded it upon the flatboat together with his carpenter tools and implements and some household goods.

He floated leisurely down the Rolling Fork and into Salt River which stream soon brought him to the broad Ohio at the place today called West Point. Embarking upon the larger stream he found the going more hazardous and soon his small craft capsized and his cargo went into the river. Recovering his tools, furniture and most of his whiskey he continued down stream tying up at Thompson's Ferry at the mouth of Anderson Creek in Indiana. Here he stored his goods and started overland on foot to find an acquaintance who had settled on Little Pigeon Creek, a distance of about eighteen miles back from the river.

The country was at the time primitive forest but the soil seemed fertile. Thomas selected a quarter section of land within the present village of Lincoln City in Spencer County, marking its corners by brush piles. Then he continued on foot to the old French town of Vincennes, sixty miles to the north-westward, to file his claim at the United States land office. This accomplished he returned to Knob Creek on foot to inform his family of his new plans.

Preparations were hastily made for removal to the new home. The season was already advanced and no time should be lost if they were to be on Little Pigeon "by the time snow flies." Doubtless there was a hasty sale of surplus stock and other articles. Tom Lincoln was a good trader. Records show that he was a successful bidder and purchaser at various sales in the Knob Creek district. In fact, like most of the men of the countryside, he habitually attended auctions. He knew how they were run. Perhaps he "sold off" the stallion and brood mares that he owned on Knob Creek, keeping only those which he wished to remove

to his new home. At any rate, the belongings were
not so plentiful as to require much time in disposition.

Just how they made the trip or what route they
took is still in dispute. There are those down in the
Rolling Fork country who maintain that they went
by boat, but that is scarcely thinkable. Their new
home was barely a hundred miles away, by the
rambling road necessary in that day. Some authors
picture a covered wagon piled high with household
effects with Nancy and her bairns atop; others picture
the party on horseback, Thomas and Nancy each
managing a child. Horses undoubtedly they took, a
cow or two, perhaps a few chickens and one or more
young pigs. As for furniture, Tom could make what
he needed when they arrived, but cooking utensils,
bedding, and clothing had to be taken.

The route from Knob Creek is still uncertain, but
it probably led over old Muldraugh, past Little Mount
burying ground where not long since Tom and Nancy
had buried that tiny bit of pink flesh in a rude wooden
box. Nancy *must* go by that way. The road doubtless
led by Hodgenville where they saw Henry and Lucy
Sparrow, Nancy's foster parents, who were soon to
follow them to their new home across the Ohio. At
Elizabethtown they probably "put up" overnight
with Joseph Hanks' family before pushing on to a
point on the Ohio opposite the mouth of Anderson
Creek where the ferry boat landed.

Arriving on the Indiana side near the little town
of Troy which was to be their new trading point, Tom
borrowed a wagon, loaded the supplies, stored a few
weeks before, and set out through the deep woods for
Little Pigeon Creek which for the next fourteen years
was to be his home. Thus closed the Kentucky
chapters of Abraham Lincoln's life. His mother was
never again to see Kentucky, and his own life was to
have but little further contact with that state, although
the best friend of his young manhood, Joshua Speed,

and the woman he was to marry were to come from Kentucky.

It is not feasible to follow the supposed route taken by the Lincolns from Elizabethtown to the Ohio. If one wishes to visit the Lincoln Country of Indiana, he can approximate the route by taking the Dixie Highway (Route 31) from Elizabethtown to Hilltop (25 miles) and thence on U. S. Route 60 westward via Brandenburg (14 miles), to Hardinsburg (29 miles) and Cannelton (22 miles). The road from Hilltop west is of gravel. At Cannelton one ferries over the Ohio, taking *Indiana Route 64*, to Tell City (3.5 miles), Troy, (3.5 miles) and on thirteen miles to intersection with Route 45, north on Route 45 to intersection with pavement (Route 62) at Bradley (4.5 miles) and Lincoln City (5.5 miles).

One can also cross the Ohio by bridge at Louisville to New Albany, Indiana. (Toll $.25 for car and $.05 per passenger) and take Route 62 to Lincoln City. This route leads through Corydon, the early capital city of Indiana (21 miles) and Leavenworth on the Ohio (18 miles). Lincoln City is about eighty-five miles from New Albany. This road, which leads through a very picturesque country, is of gravel from Lanesville west and narrow between Corydon and Leavenworth. The route through Indiana is much shorter than that on the Kentucky side. From Lincoln City to Evansville (39 miles) the highway is of concrete. From Evansville one takes the Dixie Bee Line (Route 41, concrete pavement) northward to historic Vincennes and the Lincoln Country of Illinois.

IN THE LINCOLN COUNTRY
OF INDIANA

CHAPTER V
The Lincoln Home in Indiana

THE stately Ohio is a broad stream where Anderson Creek meets its placid waters and its majestic flood must have markedly impressed the lad, not yet eight years of age, who had never before seen a river larger than the Rolling Fork. In the days when the Lincolns came to Indiana, Thompson's ferry was little better than a man-propelled, clumsy, raft-like boat which plied irregularly between the Kentucky shore and the alluvial "flat" at the mouth of Anderson Creek. Near by stood the little town of Troy which did a flourishing business in wood, the fuel of the river steamers, and had already established a trade in pork, corn, and furs. Occasionally the river boats tied up for the night at the "flat" and it was always a busy place when a boat was in. Troy continued for many years to flourish, but, with the building of the railways and the decline of river traffic, it fell almost into oblivion. It was at Troy that the future President was to gain his first knowledge of boats and waterways.

The Lincolns arrived in Indiana sometime after Thanksgiving, 1816, and Thomas set to work immediately to prepare a camp for the winter. Ordinarily the winters in southern Indiana are pleasant and open, but the winter of 1816–17 is recorded as having been uncommonly severe. Much has been made of the primitive character of this camp in the biographies of Mr. Lincoln, but it was probably not less comfortable than those rude early shelters built by the Pilgrim Fathers in a much more rigorous climate. Dennis Hanks described the shelter as a "half-faced camp." It was doubtless a shed-like porch, closed in at the

ends, backed up against a hillside which had been cut
back to make a sort of dug-out. It faced the south,
making the most of the sunshine, and was open on this
side. A blazing fire in a huge stone fireplace was kept
burning in front of the camp day and night and thus
all within kept comfortable. During the day the
labor of felling trees and getting a "clearing" open
for a spring crop kept one's blood in circulation and
left little chance for one to get cold.

That first winter was later described by Abraham
as a "pretty pinching" time but Thomas and Nancy
were not too discouraged to send to Nolin Creek good
reports on the country to the end that Thomas and
Elizabeth Sparrow, Nancy's foster parents, who were
rearing Dennis Hanks, and Dennis' own mother,
Nancy Hanks Hall, and his step-father, Levi, soon
followed them. By this time Thomas Lincoln, with
the help of neighbors and the little that Abraham could
do, had succeeded in building a permanent cabin and
the two new families enjoyed successively the uses of
the "half-face camp," and were glad to get it.

The Lincoln cabin was of hewn logs, eighteen feet
square. It had an earthen floor and a low loft reached
by wooden pegs driven into the wooden walls. At
first there were neither windows nor doors; these were
to come later but, alas, not until Nancy had passed
to the "Great Beyond" and Thomas had brought
from Kentucky a new mother for his bairns. We may
be sure that the home-loving Nancy had meanwhile
been glad to get into a permanent abode and we may
guess also that she was immediately busy "tidying
up" this new house.

But she was not long spared to her husband and
children and, within two short years after the arrival
of the family in Indiana, Nancy Hanks Lincoln was
stricken with what in southern Indiana is known as
the "milk sick." This malarial disorder found elsewhere in pioneer countries, was particularly bad in the

fall of 1818 and by October 5 the delicate mother was dead. Thomas and Elizabeth Sparrow and Levi and Nancy Hall also succumbed and thus only Thomas, Sarah, Abraham, and the boy Dennis were left of the little party so recently come from Kentucky.

This wholesale striking of the hand of death must have called for all of fortitude any man could muster, but Thomas, with his sorrowing children at his side, sawed out lumber for coffins and, with his own hands, laid to rest his friends, his relatives and his own wife. The religious convictions of the Lincolns did not call for immediate burial services, and thus it was that such rites for Nancy Hanks Lincoln and the other victims of this visitation of the epidemic were not held until the following spring.

It is a beautiful spot in which they buried the mother of the President. It is situated upon a slight knoll about a quarter of a mile south of the Lincoln cabin. Here a little cluster of graves—those of Nancy and her relatives—are to be seen in the shade of the splendid group of trees which cover the hill. Thomas could not put up a permanent memorial and it remained for friends of the family later to mark the spot. Apparently a subscription was taken up for the purpose. This simple early marker served until 1879, when Mr. Clement Studebaker, Sr., of South Bend, Indiana, had erected over the grave a beautiful but unostentatious stone with this inscription:

Nancy Hanks Lincoln,
Mother of President Lincoln,
Died October 5, A. D. 1818,
Aged 35 Years.
Erected by a friend of her
Martyred Son.

In 1902 the present monument was put up and the Studebaker marker removed to the foot of the grave, doing in my estimation, serious damage to the quiet dignity and noble simplicity of the place.

It was a desolate cabin to which the lad Abraham and his shy sister returned after their mother's burial. The taking of the dearest being he had known in life was a serious tragedy—the first of many that were to cast "lengthening shadows" across his life. But he remembered her parting words, "to be kind to his father and sister" and he tried his best. Time eventually alleviated the sharpest pangs of his sorrow, but it never quite erased for him the sadness of it all.

For a time Sarah, his sister, tried to be mother and housekeeper, but it was an uphill struggle and Thomas Lincoln soon came to realize the futility of such a scheme. They got on for a year but at the end of this time Thomas made his way back to Elizabethtown to bring home a new mother for his children. As a youth in the town he had known Sarah Bush who had married Daniel Johnston. Johnston had died several years before and of this Thomas Lincoln doubtless had information. The story still persists that earlier in life Lincoln had been a suitor for her hand. Be that as it may, once Thomas Lincoln had arrived in Elizabethtown, he was not long in convincing the widow Johnston that she should marry him and return with him to Indiana.

Mrs. Johnston was "the owner of a goodly stock of furniture and household goods" among which was a walnut bureau which she highly prized. These belongings, together with the widow and her three children, John, Sarah, and Matilda, were loaded into the spacious wagon of Ralph Crume, Tom Lincoln's brother-in-law, and by him the happy pair and their belongings were transported to their Indiana home.

"What effect the new family, their collection of furniture, cooking utensils, and comfortable bedding must have had on the astonished and motherless ones who from the door of Thomas Lincoln's forlorn cabin watched the well-filled wagon as it came creaking through the woods can better be imagined than described," says Herndon. It must have been a happy day for the lonesome boy and girl, for although none could take the place of their own sweet-faced, soft-voiced mother, the kind motherly woman whom Tom Lincoln introduced as their "new mother," immediately took the deepest interest in their welfare and adopted them as her own. Especially was she attracted to the thoughtful and obedient Abe, who so much needed a mother who understood him. And throughout her long life she testified to his sterling qualities and we know that Mr. Lincoln always cherished a real affection for her.

The new Mrs. Lincoln was an energetic, sprightly woman and with true motherly instinct she set about making the cabin a real home. She directed Thomas to get out boards for a floor, make windows and doors and securely "chink" the cracks between the logs. Her furniture and good feather ticks made the place neat and comfortable and her radiant spirit and active industry changed the lonesome cabin into a cheerful abode.

This cabin, so far as I know, was the only cabin ever built on this site by Thomas Lincoln. It was still standing as late as 1860 at which time a sketch which comes down to us was made. At that time a "lean-to" had been added at the rear and a "puncheon" floored porch crossed its front. The site of this home which the family was to occupy for thirteen years, or until they removed to Illinois, is today in the eastern limits of the little village of Lincoln City, Spencer County, which occupies the western portion of the quarter section of land that Thomas Lincoln "took up" when he made his first visit to Indiana. Later Lincoln relinquished claim to the eastern half of this tract, paying for the "eighty" to which he received patent in 1827. The village school stands immediately

west of the cabin site which is now marked by a simple
monument. This stone bears the legend:

SPENCER COUNTY
MEMORIAL
TO
ABRAHAM LINCOLN
WHO LIVED
ON THIS SPOT
FROM
1816 – 1830.

In 1907 the wooded tract immediately surrounding
the grave of the President's mother passed into the
custody of the State of Indiana and was by the state
erected into Nancy Hanks State Park. This park
approximates seventy acres in area but it does not
include the cabin site. In fact, almost thirty acres of
the original Lincoln farm lie outside the Park. Within
a few months the Indiana Lincoln Union, a public-
spirited organization of Hoosiers, has been founded
with the avowed purpose of acquiring the remainder
of the Lincoln farm, of improving the tract and of
erecting thereon a suitable shrine to the illustrious
American who there spent his boyhood. Olmsted
Brothers, the distinguished landscape architects of
Brookline, Massachusetts, have been employed to
plan the park and Mr. Thomas Hibben of New York
has been retained as architect.

The means by which one may reach Lincoln City
from Louisville have been reviewed in Chapter IV.
The Lincoln Country of Indiana is readily accessible
from the Illinois towns, Chicago, Indianapolis, or
Saint Louis. Any road from the Lincoln Country of
Illinois that intersects the Illinois State Highway
No. 1 (Dixie Highway) will lead one via Vincennes to
Evansville, Indiana, from which the Park is distant
only forty miles. Leave Evansville by Virginia Street
and Rose Avenue, taking Indiana State Highway

PROPOSED LINCOLN MEMORIAL
NANCY HANKS STATE PARK, LINCOLN CITY, INDIANA
THOMAS HIBBEN, ARCHITECT
OLMSTED BROTHERS, LANDSCAPE ARCHITECTS
By Courtesy of the Indiana Lincoln Union

No. 16 north and east via Boonville to Lincoln City.
While at Lincoln City the Lincoln admirer will want
to cover the area that Lincoln knew as a boy and visit
the places connected with important episodes of his
early life.

When Thomas got the farm pretty well under way
with the help of Abe and John Johnston, the boys
could be released to be "hired out" to the neighbors.
The usual wage was twenty-five cents a day, and since
Abe was skillful with the axe and knew some of the
principles of carpentry, as well as how to do farm
work, his services were in demand throughout the
countryside. It is told of him that he often read between plowing rows of corn and later at night before
the fire after the family had retired.

We know something of the books that he read as a
youth and among them one notes "Pilgrim's Progress,"
"Aesop's Fables," "Robinson Crusoe" and Parson
Weem's "Life of Washington," each and every one of
them books we have all loved as boys. In the matter
of early literature, Lincoln was not so badly off, it
seems to me. He devoured books so rapidly, however,
that he constantly needed new material upon which
to whet his mind. Of course the Bible was always at
hand in his own home but for livelier reading he
scoured the country round about, borrowing from
friends in Rockport, Troy, and Boonville.

The visitor to the section will be shown near
Gentryville the site of the first Indiana school attended
by Lincoln and the site of Jones' general store. Abe
was often here and at the mill not far away. In those
days corn for meal had to be taken to the mill, which
was operated in damp weather by water but in the dry
days of summer by horse power. In later life Mr.
Lincoln often recalled the days at mill.

"The centre of wit and wisdom in the village of
Gentryville was at the store," says Herndon, and Abe
loved to loaf at the store. Under similar circumstances

I think most boys would. There the inquiring mind
would hear discussed the current questions of the day,
and to take part in such discussion would be to assume
a man's place. Then there was another attraction, for
the storekeeper received a Louisville newspaper and
the lad was eager to devour its contents and talk with
others upon the questions it raised in his mind.

The young man liked to attend trials before the
local "squire" and often attended "court" in the
neighboring county-seat towns of Boonville, fifteen
miles southwest on the road to Evansville, and Rockport, the seat of Spencer County, seventeen miles south
of his home. The old court houses that stood in his
time have either burned or been pulled down, but, as
in his day, justice is still dispensed here. In the court
house at Rockport there is displayed a cupboard or
cabinet that purports to have been made by Tom
Lincoln with perhaps the help of his son, and owners
of several houses in the county boast that their homes
were in part at least constructed by the Lincolns.

At Boonville Lincoln heard the astounding oratory
of a rising lawyer by the name of Breckenridge which,
according to his testimony after he became President,
was the most brilliant utterance that he had up to that
time heard, and at Rockport he came to know John
Pitcher, one of the great lawyers of the day. Judge
Pitcher afterward testified that the young man borrowed many a book from his library.

One will want to go to Rockport not only for its
Lincoln interest, but also for its picturesque scenery,
the sheer rock cliffs above the town, the site of the old
ferry landing from which Lincoln embarked in the
spring of 1828 on his first flatboat trip to New Orleans,
and for the splendid views of the Ohio. The old hotel
in Rockport where Lincoln is reported to have stayed
when he revisited the county in 1844, campaigning
for Henry Clay, is still pointed out.

The visitor will also wish to go to Pigeon Creek

Church where the Lincolns worshipped and of which Thomas and Sarah Bush Lincoln were members. This church was not in existence when the Lincolns first arrived from Kentucky and Thomas and Abraham are said to have labored upon the structure. Thomas Lincoln's name often appears upon the records of the organization where he appears to have served as "moderator." The churchyard is a picturesque spot and among the stones will be found that of Abraham's sister Sarah who married Aaron Grigsby in 1826. According to the records in the Lincoln family bible (Gunther Collection, Chicago) Sarah died January 20, 1828.

A trip to the little river town of Troy is not without interest also. It was here that, during his later days in Indiana, Lincoln was employed by James Taylor, the owner of the store in the town, to operate a ferry boat across Anderson Creek. Anderson Creek was a familiar spot to Abe for it was here that he first set foot on Indiana soil. It was while so engaged (1826) that Lincoln's first actual contact with the law came about.

It seems that the Ohio River ferry was at the time operated by Dill Brothers, who had a license to propel trans-river craft. However, often when their ferry was upon the opposite bank, young Lincoln used to pick up a bit of business with his own flat-bottomed boat. It so happened that, in order to accommodate some people who desired to reach an Ohio River steamer that stood in the middle of the stream, Lincoln took them out in his own boat. The story goes, according to Secretary Seward, that when Abe had seen them safely upon the boat one of the party threw down to him a silver dollar, the equivalent of about three days wages, as he was being paid at the time.

Abe was very much pleased but was soon to have the joy taken out of the event as he was immediately charged by Dill Brothers with operating a ferry without a license. He was served with a warrant from Samuel Pate, a Kentucky Justice of the Peace, and went before that official to plead his own case. Admitting the facts, he denied having infringed the rights of Dill Brothers or having violated the law. His argument was that he was *not* operating a ferry, inasmuch as he did not transport any one *across the stream* but only *to midstream*. Justice Pate rendered a decision in favor of the defendant but advised him to "read up a bit on the law." This is the first court record in which the name of Abraham Lincoln appears. Evidently he took Squire Pate's suggestion, for soon afterward he borrowed a copy of the "Revised Statutes of Indiana" from his friend David Turnham and made himself master of its contents. This is believed to have been the first such book he ever read and the arrest appears to have been a fortunate happening in that it directed Lincoln's attention to a study of the law.

IN THE LINCOLN COUNTRY OF ILLINOIS

CHAPTER VI
The Journey to Illinois—Lincoln Way

THE autumn of 1829 saw a recurrence of the same disease which eleven years before had carried off Lincoln's mother and her kinsmen. None of the Lincoln family fell in this epidemic but many of their neighbors succumbed and everyone lost cattle. Several years before this, William Hanks (see page 36) with his family had moved from Kentucky to Macon County, Illinois, settling five miles northwest of the town of Decatur. He had reported the Illinois country good land, but to make sure that the report was valid Dennis Hanks, who had married Sarah, the daughter of Sarah Bush Lincoln, made a trip to Illinois to look up a location and advise as to conditions. His report was favorable and so the Lincolns and their relatives decided to remove to that state.

Thomas then owned eighty acres of land, to which he had obtained patent two years before. Selling this, his stock and grain, he paid his debts and on the first day of March, 1830, set out with his family and relatives for Illinois. The party included Thomas and Sarah Bush Lincoln, Abraham Lincoln and his stepbrother, John D. Johnston, Dennis Hanks, his wife Sarah and four children, Matilda, another daughter of Sarah Bush Lincoln, her husband, Squire Hall, and one son, John—a party of thirteen souls.* How many wagons the party had is not quite plain. Some accounts mention three wagons, two drawn by oxen and one drawn by horses, others say two wagons and some but one wagon.

* Thompson, "Investigation of the Lincoln Way," 30. Affidavit of Harriet Hanks Chapman, daughter of Dennis Hanks and one of the party.

At this time highways in anything like the modern sense were unknown and what roads there were were little better than trails "up hill and down dale" until the Wabash River was reached. The country upon the Illinois side of that stream is less broken, but even here roads, however primitive, were scarce and there were as yet no bridges. The National Road had then only been surveyed and no bridges or grading had been completed. Worst of all, at this season of the year the streams were swollen and, where the frost had left the ground, there was "no bottom" to the road. Fortunately, for a large part of the way the soil was still frozen, although the surface "muddied up" during the day.

Colonel Chapman of Charleston, Illinois, who married Harriett Hanks, gives us some data regarding the party. He says, "Thomas Lincoln moved from Indiana to Illinois in a large four horse wagon drawn by two yoke of oxen; only wagon he ever owned; brought with him some stock cattle; one horse; three beds and bedding; one bureau; one table; one set chairs; cooking utensils, etc. There were three families together: Lincolns, Halls, and Hanks. . . . Abe Lincoln drove his father's ox team. The waters were very high at the time and they came near losing their team, wagon and contents in crossing the Okaw or Kaskaskia river."*

There has long existed tradition and "hearsay" regarding the departure of the Lincoln party and the route it took in coming to Illinois. Many of these statements are irreconcilable, so irreconcilable in fact that today a large part of the so-called "Lincoln route" is in dispute. In December, 1916, a commission appointed by Governor Samuel M. Ralston of Indiana rendered a report which located the "official" route from Lincoln City through Dale, Jasper, and Peters-

* Thompson, Op. Cit., 34.

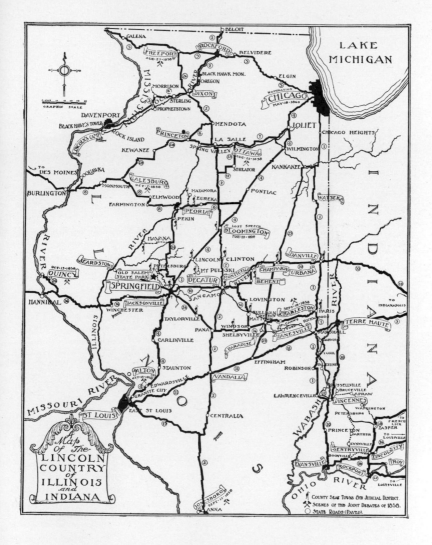

A Map of The LINCOLN COUNTRY of ILLINOIS and INDIANA

burg to Vincennes. (See route on map, page 76). This route was apparently not received as conclusive by people in other parts of the Lincoln country of Indiana and I have before me a paper prepared by William L. Barker of Boonville, Indiana, which attempts to show that the party passed from Lincoln City to Boonville in Warrick County and from here via Lynnville and Arthur to Petersburg. (See dotted line on map, page 76). He introduces a number of sworn statements to support his theory. Thus the merry war over the route taken by this good pioneer family goes on. Let us hope that all this discussion may result in the identification of the actual country traversed by them.

Illinois has been no less dilatory in the matter of attempting to locate the route taken by the family in *that* state, and in 1916 Dr. Charles M. Thompson of the University of Illinois published a report upon the subject. After digesting the testimony of living members of the Lincoln party, what evidence could be drawn from Mr. Lincoln's recorded utterances upon the subject, evidence regarding old roads of the time, and tradition in the various communities through which the party is supposed to have passed, something like the route the party must have taken was determined. In several parts of the journey great uncertainty still exists, however, and many people here, as in Indiana, are not ready to accept the findings of the investigator.

One of the important documents bearing upon this question is reported by Jesse W. Weik, who in January, 1896, interviewed Colonel Augustus H. Chapman and his wife, Harriett, the daughter of Dennis Hanks. This interview, published by Dr. Thompson in his "The Investigation of the Lincoln Way," is as follows:

Charleston, Illinois,
January 3, 1896.

Colonel Augustus H. Chapman: married daughter of
Dennis Hanks and latter has been living with us off and on
for many years; have often talked with him about the
journey from Indiana to Illinois in 1830; also with Sarah
Bush Lincoln, his mother-in-law, who also lived in my family
for some time prior to her death in 1869. Late in January,
1861, when Mr. Lincoln came to Charleston to visit his
stepmother, I rode with him to the graveyard in the country
where his father was buried; he had spent the previous night
at my house where the old lady then lived. We got to talk-
ing about the journey from Indiana in 1830; he agreed substantially with Hanks as to the route they took; said they
went from Gentryville to Jasper in Dubois county; thence to
Washington, Daviess county; thence to Vincennes, where
they crossed the Wabash; thence towards Lawrenceville,
where they turned north and pushed on to Palestine in
Crawford county. At Palestine they found a great many
people drawn there by the land office. They kept on north
paralleling the river to Darwin, where they left the Wabash
behind them. At this point, they set off in a northwest-
wardly direction, passing through Richwoods in Clark
county; thence to a point about six miles west of Charleston
called Dead Man's Grove, thence north through Nelsonville,
Moultrie county to Decatur, where they stopped."

Dr. Thompson[*] also includes an affidavit of Mrs.
Harriett Chapman, daughter of Dennis Hanks, and a
member of the party. Since Mrs. Chapman was a
child not more than four years old at the time, her
testimony is based largely upon what has come down
as tradition in her family. She states "that the party
in leaving Vincennes went by land, camped the first
night out near a grist mill; that the party crossed the
Wabash River the next day (the second day after
leaving Vincennes, Indiana)." She further stated
"that the party passed through Palestine, Illinois;
that she remembers said town from the fact that it had

[*] Op. Cit. 30.

a Bible name," and further "that the party finally reached the national road, and crossed the Embarras River at Greenup, Illinois; passed through Paradise, located in what is now the southwestern corner of Coles County, Illinois . . . that the party did not follow the national road far west of Greenup, that it did not go to Vandalia, Illinois, and that the trip was made directly to Decatur."

In view of such conflicting testimony as the two accounts above given it will be seen that the matter of locating the actual route taken by the party becomes exceedingly difficult. In the matter of the crossing at Vincennes Mrs. Chapman's testimony seems to be corroborated by that of James Wade Emison and others of Indiana which Dr. Thompson also includes.* These statements seem to indicate that the Lincoln party approached Vincennes from the east, crossing the White River at the Apraw ford and coming west into Vincennes, then north to Bruceville and again west, crossing into Illinois at the Russellville ford of the Wabash. (This route is marked by a broken line on map, page 76).

An affidavit of William J. Trout indicates that the old road of those days ran through Pike and Daviess counties, crossing the White River at Apraw ford, and continued west into Bruceville. The present-day road from Apraw to Bruceville strikes the Vincennes-Bruceville Road (See map on page 76) at a point between Vincennes and Bruceville. If this road in any way parallels the old road it would seem that in coming from Washington, as Mr. Lincoln stated, the party may have crossed the White at Apraw, continued west to the junction of the Apraw road with the Vincennes-Bruceville Road, turned into Vincennes to trade and ask directions, then continued north to Bruceville, camping at Emison mill on Mariah Creek

* Ibid, 23-29.

and continuing on to the Russellville ford on the
Wabash.

Colonel Chapman, however, quotes Mr. Lincoln
as saying that the party crossed the Wabash at Vincennes, and since Mr. Lincoln was at the time twenty-
one years of age and drove the oxen pulling one of the
wagons, his testimony would outweigh that of others.
On our map, therefore, the route named by Mr. Lincoln is shown in a solid black line, the disputed or
other possible routes in dotted lines or dashes.

"After crossing the Wabash at Vincennes," says
Dr. Thompson in his report, "the Lincolns went westward along the great western mail route to Lawrenceville. At that point they turned northward, going to
Palestine in Crawford county." Near Lawrenceville,
where a strong local tradition still persists regarding
the passage of the Lincolns through the town, the
party, according to Dr. Thompson, ferried the Embarras River and took a northeasternly direction to the
Christian settlement on the Allison prairie. They then
continued on this road until they reached the "river
road" at or near Russellville. The river road paralleled
the Wabash and this the party followed northward to
Palestine, Hutsonville, York, and Darwin, then the
county seat of Clark County.

From Darwin their route lay to the northwestward
through the Richwoods settlement (about three miles
east of the present town of Westfield, Clark County),
thence slightly southwestwardly to cross the Embarras
at McCann's ford and on westward and a little north
to the Paradise settlement near the present town of
Mattoon. Here, according to the tradition in the
Hall family, they sought friends who had moved from
Kentucky. This family was that of Ichabod Radley,
the Elizabethtown schoolmaster. (See page 43.)
Dr. Thompson affirms that the Radleys were living in
the Paradise settlement at the time but that Ichabod
Radley did not own land in Coles County until later.

The Paradise neighborhood is today the location of a resort known as Paradise Lake.

According to Mr. Lincoln the party went next to Dead Man's Grove, a short distance northeast of the present site of the city of Mattoon. From this neighborhood they traveled in a northwesternly direction to Nelsonville, identified with Nelson, a village located about five miles southeast of Sullivan, Moultrie County, and not far from the present town of Allenville. About here occurred the near disaster that accompanied the fording of the Kaskaskia River.

From this point the way is not plain, but Mr. Lincoln is quoted as having said in after life that, so far as he was then able to reconstruct their route, it lay not far from the course at present taken by the Illinois Central Railroad from Sullivan to Decatur. Some would take the party through Lovington, but regarding this route we have practically no evidence. It is generally assumed that the Lincolns approached the recently plotted (1829) town of Decatur from the south, but for this also there is little evidence. That they stopped in Decatur is well authenticated. Major Henry C. Whitney in his "Life on the Circuit with Lincoln" tells of Mr. Lincoln's remarks upon one occasion when with a group of men he was standing near the court house square in Decatur. "After supper," says the Major, "we strolled out for a walk and when we came to the court house Lincoln walked out a few steps in front and after shifting his position two or three times he said, as he looked up at the building. . . . 'Here is the exact spot where I stood by our wagon when we moved from Indiana twenty-six years ago; this isn't six feet from the exact spot.'"

The original log court house which had only recently been built when the Lincolns first saw Decatur is still preserved for us and stands today upon a pretty eminence in Fairview Park. This two story log structure, built in 1829, served as the seat of government for Macon county for ten years. It bears a bronze tablet with this legend:

IN THIS MACON COUNTY'S
FIRST COURT HOUSE
BUILT IN 1829
ABRAHAM LINCOLN
PRACTISED LAW WHILE ON
THE EIGHTH JUDICIAL DISTRICT.

———

THIS TABLET PLACED BY THE LINCOLN
MEMORIAL COMMITTEE OF THE
ASSOCIATION OF COMMERCE, DECATUR.

Inasmuch as Mr. Lincoln did not practise law before 1837, it will be seen that he can have made very few if any pleas in this structure. It was in 1839 replaced by a nobler seat of justice.

John Hanks, son of William Hanks and born in Kentucky about 1802, had come to Illinois in 1826 or 27. He married Susan Wilson* in Kentucky and, coming to Macon County, had settled in the Stevens' settlement about five miles northwest of the court house at Decatur. Meeting the Lincolns in Decatur, "he sheltered them until they were safely housed on a piece of land which he had selected for them five miles further westward."

"The place he had selected," says Herndon, "was a bluff overlooking the Sangamon river—for these early settlers must always be in sight of a running stream—well supplied with timber. It was a charming and picturesque site, and all hands set resolutely to work to prepare the new abode. One felled trees; one hewed the timbers for the cabin; while another cleared the ground of its accumulated growth of underbrush." Thomas Lincoln doubtless superintended the construction of the cabin, while John and Abe, with the aid of the oxen, broke up some fifteen acres of virgin

* Smith, "History of Macon County, Illinois," 262.

URBANA-LINCOLN HOTEL, URBANA, ILLINOIS
On the site of the old Kerr Tavern

EARLY COURT-HOUSE AT DECATUR, ILLINOIS
In use when the Lincolns arrived from Indiana

Photographs by the Author

prairie sod, making it ready for cultivation. John
Hanks records that "Abe and myself split rails enough
to fence the place in."

Abe Lincoln remained in the vicinity of Decatur
for about a year, working "at odd jobs" in the neighborhood, or wherever the demand for his services
called him. He had, however, attained his majority
and was now his own man. Hanks records that in
1830–31 Lincoln made three thousand rails for Major
Warnick, meanwhile reading all the books obtainable
and practising speaking upon all available occasions.
One such address, Hanks tells us, was upon the question of "the navigation of the Sangamon River."

In the vicinity ague, chills and fever, or the "Illinois
shakes," as it was variously called, was prevalent every
fall and at this season everybody was miserable. The
Lincolns did not like this situation and, according to
Mrs. Sarah Jane Dowling, a daughter of Dennis Hanks,
had been in Macon County a little over a year "when
the chills and fever were so bad that they became discouraged and started back to Indiana. . . . In the
meantime," continues Mrs. Dowling, "Abraham Lincoln had left the party and started out in life for himself.
Arriving at Wabash Point, where Mattoon now is,
they came across two families, the Sawyers and Radleys
. . . and these people induced them to remain in Coles
County. Thomas Lincoln located eight miles south
of Charleston and lived there the rest of his life with
the exception of two years that he and Dennis Hanks
ran a grist mill on the Embarras River. . . . Thomas
moved back to the old home place, where he died in
1851, and is buried in the old Gordon graveyard, one
and one-half miles west." Sarah Bush Lincoln died
in 1869 while she was residing at the old home place
with the family of John J. Hall.

The Gordon Cemetery mentioned above, as well
as the Lincoln farm in Coles County, lies upon what is
locally known as Goosenest prairie. It is not far from

McCann's ford where the Lincoln party crossed the Embarras in coming from Indiana. The old Lincoln cabin has now disappeared but in the Gordon Cemetery are to be seen monuments marking the burial places of the President's father and mother. The stone over the father's grave, although he died in 1851, was not placed until after the assassination of his illustrious son. It bears this inscription:

THOMAS LINCOLN, FATHER OF
THE MARTYRED PRESIDENT.
BORN JAN. 6, 1778.
DIED JAN. 15, 1851.

———

LINCOLN

———

For many years the grave of Sarah Bush Lincoln lay neglected and unmarked, but in 1924 the Lions Clubs of Illinois erected a dignified monument of Barre granite above her resting place. It bears this inscription:

THOMAS AND SARAH BUSH LINCOLN
1778–1851   1788–1869
FATHER AND STEPMOTHER OF OUR MARTYRED
PRESIDENT

———

Their Humble but Worthy Home Gave to the World
ABRAHAM LINCOLN

———

Erected by the Lions Clubs of the State of Illinois.

———

The road to Gordon Cemetery, which lies adjacent to old Shiloh Presbyterian Church and which is a very pretty spot, leads south and east from Mattoon (See map). Leave Mattoon passing the Country Club and taking the road for Janesville via Lerna. Signboards on the Lerna-Janesville road before reaching Janes-

MONUMENT TO THOMAS AND SARAH BUSH LINCOLN

TOMBSTONE OVER GRAVE OF THOMAS LINCOLN

NEAR JANESVILLE, ILLINOIS

Photographs by the Author

ville point the way to Gordon Cemetery which is about a mile and a half northeast of Janesville. The distance from Mattoon is twelve miles but the road is not paved. It is, however, well oiled and ordinarily in excellent condition.

CHAPTER VII

New Salem and Lincoln

IF DECATUR and Macon County were the scenes of Lincoln's first residence in Illinois he was not long to remain here. The winter of 1830–31 is still known as the winter of the "Deep Snow" in central Illinois, and during that season Lincoln with John Hanks split rails for Major Warnick in the vicinity of Decatur. Toward the latter part of the winter Denton Offut, "a brisk and venturesome business man," came to the neighborhood to engage John Hanks to take a boatload of stock and provisions to New Orleans. Driving a bargain with Offut, Hanks introduced Lincoln and Lincoln's stepbrother, John Johnston, whom he wished to assist him on the trip. Terms were agreed upon and Offut set out for Springfield promising to have the boat ready when the boatmen should arrive at Beardstown in the spring.

Lincoln and Hanks descended the Sangamon in March, landing at Judy's Ferry near the present village of Jamestown. Walking to Springfield to look up Offut they found that the boat was not ready, and that, as a matter of fact, it had not as yet been built. The three young men, somewhat disappointed at this turn of affairs, agreed, however, to construct the boat and presently set about procuring the timber from public lands nearby. At a small village then known as Sangamo Town there was a sawmill and since this was near the timber, the village was selected as the place to build the boat. There now exists no vestige of this little town which, incorporated in 1824, was located seven miles northwest of Springfield on the banks of the Sangamon River, but Roll's Ford on

that stream is not far from the spot where Lincoln and
his associates constructed the boat in the spring of
1831. Nearby today is Camp Colgan, the resort of
the Catholic Boy's Brigade.

It required four weeks to complete the craft and
the event of its launching created considerable interest
in the countryside, as it was the first step toward the
building up of a river commerce so much advocated in
those days. A prosperous and energetic trader like
Denton Offut was expected to do much for the encouragement of such an enterprise. John Linden Roll
in the Journal of the Illinois State Historical Society
(Vol. XIX) recounts several incidents connected with
the building of this flatboat and records that John
Eddy Roll, Walter Carman, John Seaman, and "a
man by the name of Cabanis" assisted in building
the craft. Mr. Roll says that his father, the John
Eddy Roll above mentioned, visited the former site of
Sangamo Town "sixty-one years after he had worked
there with Lincoln" and that "without much trouble
he located . . . . the exact spot on the bank of the
river, where the flatboat was constructed and launched.
An old sawmill stood there and was used in sawing
lumber for the boat. The spot on which the mill stood
seems to have been washed away. It was a low, flat
strip of land along the river . . . . and the stream
made great inroads on it."

The boat was loaded with grain, barreled pork and
hogs, and about the middle of April the party started
it down the Sangamon toward Beardstown where it
was to embark upon the broader course of the Illinois
River. On April 19, the loaded craft hung up on the
mill-dam at the little village of New Salem, twenty
miles northwest of Springfield. Here the Sangamon,
"winding its devious way" from the south and east,
strikes a bluff that deflects its current abruptly northward and just at this point Rutledge and Cameron had

in 1829 built a dam and a combination grist and saw-mill.

During the period of construction of the boat the river had been considerably swollen by the melting snow and spring rains, but by the time New Salem was

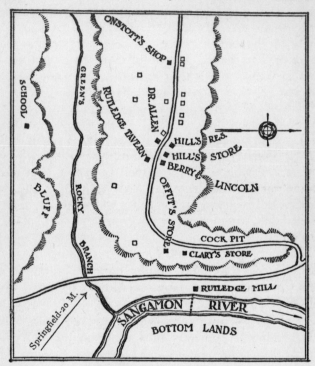

MAP OF NEW SALEM, ILLINOIS

reached the water had receded to a point where the boat could not clear the obstruction and stranded with the prow protruding beyond the dam and the stern fast and shipping water. The cargo was hastily shifted to the prow to weight down the front end while the stern was propped to prevent the boat from slipping backward. Then the cargo was transferred to the ferry boat near by. The problem now was to remove the water and thus float the boat over the dam.

"The population of New Salem," says Thomas P.
Reep, "was out in mass to watch the proceedings.
Lincoln asked for an auger and was directed to the
cooper shop of Henry Onstott. Here he secured what
he was looking for and, on his way back, cut a limb
from a tree and fashioned a plug about the diameter
of the auger bit. Back at the scene of action he bored
a hole in the bottom of the boat where it hung over
the dam and called for volunteers to stand in the
prow to weight down that end and cause the water to
flow out through the hole he had bored. When the
water was substantially all out and buoyancy restored
the boat lifted and slipped over the dam, during
which time Lincoln plugged the hole he had made.
The flat was then reloaded and the voyagers passed
on down the river." This was Lincoln's first intro-
duction to New Salem. In the light of subsequent
events one wonders how history might have been
changed had there been no dam in the Sangamon at
this point.

Lincoln, Johnston, and Offut continued the trip to
New Orleans but John Hanks left the party at St.
Louis, returning to his home in Macon County. It is
said Offut disposed of his cargo to good advantage and
that, while awaiting an up-river packet upon which
to return home, Lincoln and Johnston availed themselves of an opportunity to see the Crescent City.
Coming one day upon a slave auction they saw the
auctioneer tear open "the dresses of comely mulatto
girls to expose their persons as he extolled their good
points and bodily perfections." It is said this so in-
censed Lincoln that the expression attributed to him
in every schoolbook here escaped his lips; "If I ever
get a chance to hit that thing, I'll hit it hard."

Returning to St. Louis about the beginning of
July a letter informed Lincoln that his parents had
removed to Coles County and with Johnston he set

out for their home. But Denton Offut had determined to establish a store in the growing village of
New Salem and had employed young Lincoln to
operate it for him. After buying a stock of goods in
St. Louis, Offut took an Illinois River boat for Beardstown. Arriving there he went overland to Springfield
by stage and on July 8, 1831, secured a license from
the Sangamon County commissioners court to operate
a retail store in New Salem. He then obtained a lot on
Main Street preparatory to the erection of a log building in which to conduct his business.

Lincoln remained for a few weeks with his parents
on Goosenest prairie and arrived in New Salem about
the first of August, 1831. The village was a straggling
collection of log structures along a winding road that
led from the mill and dam on the river up the crest of
a graceful bluff that thrusts a salient bent arm toward
the river at this point. The bluff, a full hundred feet
above the level of the river and covered with oak,
ash, hickory, locust, sycamore, hawthorne, sumac,
and wild smilax, is today a lovely spot and must then
have had a certain rustic charm. A distinct contrast
it offered to the flatter prairie lands of Coles and Macon
Counties and resembled more nearly the kind of
country Lincoln had known in southern Indiana.
With its splendid views across ravine and hill, wood-
land and river, the place must have had an effect upon
the thoughtful Lincoln.

New Salem had been established in the autumn of
1828 by the Reverend John M. Cameron and his
uncle-by-marriage, James Rutledge. These serious-
minded Cumberland Presbyterians were millwrights
and had first settled on Concord Creek some seven
miles north of New Salem, where they expected to
erect a mill. When the water failed in the creek during
the summer months they transferred their activities
to the site of New Salem and there began the town

which Reuben S. Harrison surveyed and laid out for them in October, 1829.

Thus when Lincoln arrived the town was scarcely three years old, but the mill, noted above, was in operation, the Rutledge Tavern where he was to meet the sweet-faced Ann, the daughter of the family, was the village hostelry, a post office had been established and the town boasted several infant industries. The first store had been opened in 1829 by Hill and McNeil, the latter of whom we are eventually to know as John McNamar, and Samuel Hill was appointed the first postmaster. The town, which was the first post office and first platted town in that part of Sangamon, now known as Menard County, was centrally located with respect to other settlements of the district. Clary's Grove, with the inhabitants of which Lincoln was later to become acquainted, was about five miles southwest; Athens was some seven miles southeast. There were settlements also at Indian Point about seven miles east, at Sugar Grove some ten miles northeast and on Sand Ridge seven miles north. Offut believed the place destined to a good future, especially if navigation on the Sangamon succeeded.

Arriving during the absence of Offut and before the receipt of the stock of goods, Lincoln took the opportunity to get acquainted with the villagers. Just at this time the August election occurred and, in the absence of an assistant clerk, Lincoln qualified for the position and thus at once made himself of value to the community. Under the law he could and did vote here, exercising for the first time in his life his right of franchise. Among others he voted for Jack Armstrong of Clary's Grove whom later he was to meet in a wrestling combat. At length Offut returned and Lincoln assisted in getting the store building constructed and the goods installed. It was while he was employed in this store that the many little events which testify to the sterling honesty of Lincoln took place. These incidents which gave him the name of "Honest Abe" are recounted in every schoolbook and need not be recalled here.

Go to New Salem today, or as it is now called "Old Salem State Park" and you will be able to identify most of the spots connected with this interesting period of Lincoln's life, for, through the research work of the Old Salem Lincoln League, the depressions made along the forgotten streets by the foundations of the houses of the one-time flourishing village have been discovered and the State of Illinois has already done much to restore the place to something of its old aspect.

The best way to reach the Park, which so recently as 1919 became, through the generosity of Mr. William Randolph Hearst, the property of the state, is by way of Petersburg, two miles away. Petersburg, the seat of Menard County, is reached by Illinois State Highway No. 24 from Springfield (30 miles). This route leads to Peoria and Chicago as well. One may also reach the Park by going west from Springfield on the Beardstown Road (west on Jefferson Street) to Bradforton. At the schoolhouse west of the town turn right and follow the markers over an oiled road to New Salem. In inclement weather it is inadvisable to take this road, although it is the historic road trod by Lincoln himself.

At the Park, Offut's store is restored on its original site, and just below it and across the road is the site of the old cock-pit where the local sportsmen matched their fighting birds. It was in front of Offut's store that the famous wrestling encounter between Lincoln and Jack Armstrong, the bully of Clary's Grove, took place. One of the Clarys had opened a "grocery" just below Offut's store on the main street. The principal item of trade at this store was whiskey and the place was the rendezvous of the Clary's Grove crowd whenever they came to town. It seems that Mr. Offut, confident of Lincoln's physical strength,

THE OFFUT STORE
Old Salem State Park, near Petersburg, Illinois
The scene of the Lincoln-Armstrong Wrestling-match

THE MAIN STREET OF SALEM, OLD SALEM STATE PARK
Offut's store in the distance

Photographs by the Author

bragged that his clerk could "outrun, outlift or out-wrestle" anyone in the neighborhood. William Clary, the proprietor of the saloon, took the challenge for his champion and a match was arranged. Lincoln was reluctant to participate in the engagement but at length assented. He learned of the trick by which Armstrong usually conquered and saw to it that Armstrong never succeeded in getting close enough to accomplish a "hold." Angered at this, Armstrong tried to "foul" Abe, but Lincoln picked him up bodily and pitched him over his shoulder. It might have been necessary to fight Armstrong's backers but Jack Armstrong was enough of a man to acknowledge defeat and Lincoln then and there became a hero in the eyes of the Clary's Grove boys.

Soon after Offut opened his store, he leased the mill of Rutledge and Cameron, operating it in connection with the store. Lincoln had a great deal to do with the running of the mill and if you look close you will discover the traces of the old path that led off from the main road near the store and descended the bluff to the mill.

The store itself is a small structure and we may be sure it could hold only a very small stock of goods, but life was simple in such pioneer communities and the farm supplied most of what the people needed. Such emporiums sold tea, coffee, sugar, salt and whiskey, blue calico, brown muslin, home-made "jeans" and gloves, cotton chain, and straw hats, with perhaps a few ladies' bonnets and other simple apparel in the way of dry goods.

In those days money was not plentiful and it was customary to do a large credit business, furnishing the settler with goods until such time as his crops were gathered and taking the products in payment. Lincoln not being acquainted with the financial ability of the store's patrons, did not know whom to trust. Offut therefore employed a young man, who *did* know, to assist at the store. This was William Green who later bought the Radford stock of goods which he sold to Lincoln and Berry when the future President essayed the role of village merchant in his own name.

The road that leads up the hill at New Salem has recently been cut down so that the grade is much easier than it was in Lincoln's time. One may now drive up the long road to the sturdy stone museum, built in 1921, that stands not far from the old Rutledge Tavern, now restored. Follow that road, originally New Salem's "Main Street," to the museum and examine the many interesting relics of the old New Salem days and Lincoln's connection therewith. Among other things you will see the Rutledge family Bible with the record of Ann's birth, the teapot used in the Rutledge Inn, Lincoln letters and plats of his surveys in the neighborhood, the auger from the cooper's shop with which Abe bored the hole in the flat-boat when it lodged upon the dam, Ann Rutledge's side-saddle, the piano used at Lincoln's wedding, and hundreds of other mementoes of Lincoln's days in the flourishing village. The verandah at the rear of the museum, as indeed the grassy knoll in front of it, commands a charming view of the countryside.

But you will want to visit the restored buildings of the village, and the first and nearest of these is the Rutledge Inn where Lincoln boarded and wooed that lass about whom so much has lately been written. The tavern as restored is a long simple log house with a loft and ladder. It served at once as the Rutledge residence and a tavern, but it is difficult to see how it could ever have entertained many guests. Originally there were three rooms below and a large room in the loft. It is said that all the men slept upstairs. Lincoln apparently did not lodge here until his return from the Black Hawk War. Green says that he slept in the Offut store when he first arrived in the town, boarding with Rowan Herndon or John M. Cameron. The house is described by old settlers as having been made of logs but covered with clapboards upon the outside. It is said to have had a fireplace at either end and stood with its long dimension east and west. The Inn was probably the first house built at New Salem and was the last to remain. The Rutledges conducted the Inn from 1829 until 1833, at which time they moved to a farm a mile north of Concord. For many years it was occupied by Jacob Bole, who continued to reside at the place after the decline of New Salem's prosperity. The building was restored by the Old Salem Lincoln League in 1918.

Perhaps the structure next in importance because of Lincoln's connection with it is the Lincoln-Berry store north of Main Street and not far from the tavern. Upon his return from the Black Hawk War in the latter part of July, 1832, Lincoln entered into a campaign for election to the Illinois legislature. His opponent was the famous Methodist preacher, Peter Cartwright. Election day was not far off and Lincoln had little time to prepare, but he made several speeches, his first at Pappsville and one in Springfield. He was defeated, however, although in his own precinct he polled 277 of the 290 votes cast. Offut's store having "petered out," as Lincoln put it, and having been defeated in the election, he was under necessity of finding a position. No such position was open. However, Rowan Herndon, a brother of Lincoln's later law partner and biographer, desired to dispose of his interest in the firm of Herndon and Berry, and Lincoln purchased his share, giving in payment his promissory note. Thus Lincoln became a merchant in the village.

But New Salem had too many stores in proportion to the population. Moreover, the anticipated commerce upon the Sangamon, in which Lincoln and New Salem still believed did not materialize in spite of the fact that in the spring of 1832 Lincoln had himself, at the request of the captain of the *Talisman*, piloted that steamboat up the Sangamon from Beardstown to Springfield.

The coming of the *Talisman* to New Salem marked the climax of the "river days" of that village, but the optimistic promoters of the time did not then realize it. It was currently thought that navigation was practical; Lincoln shared the idea and advocated it in his campaign announcement of March, 1832. It is a historic fact that the steamer *Talisman*, purchased at Cincinnati by Captain A. Vincent Bogue, did actually ascend the river to a point near Springfield and that later the *Utility*, another river boat, reached the dam at New Salem. There was a great celebration at Springfield in honor of the arrival of the *Talisman* and Captain Bogue was fêted and dined, but the arrival there of the boat did not in any wise prove that navigation of the stream was practicable. Prosperity did *not* follow in the wake of the demonstration, and New Salem, like many another river village, from then on declined. Lincoln knew the place during its heyday.

About the time that Lincoln became a merchant in the village Crisman Brothers failed and James Rutledge was forced to take a portion of their stock of groceries upon a debt. These he sold to Lincoln and Berry. Shortly afterward Reuben Radford incurred the enmity of the Clary's Grove boys and sold his stock of goods to William Green who, the same day, resold to Lincoln and Berry. They removed their stock into this building, thus combining the stocks of three stores and eliminating all competitors but Samuel Hill.

Even then, however, Lincoln and Berry's venture did not bring the returns anticipated. "A considerable part of the stock purchased by them from their predecessors," says Thomas P. Reep,* "consisted of liquors, and because of Lincoln's prejudice against its sale and use had hindered the disposal thereof to an

---

* "Lincoln at New Salem," 47.

LINCOLN MUSEUM
Old Salem State Park, near Petersburg, Illinois

THE LINCOLN-BERRY GROCERY STORE
Old Salem State Park

Photographs by the Author

appreciable extent, their failing circumstances gave Berry the opportunity he craved and, being the senior partner, he applied for and secured in the name of Berry & Lincoln, a license to keep a tavern, which means solely in this case, the right to sell liquor by the drink." Not long afterward Lincoln, tired of the arrangement, sold his interest to Berry, taking Berry's notes in payment. Berry in turn sold to Trent Brothers, who later left, leaving their notes to Berry unpaid. Berry died insolvent and Lincoln, honest man that he was, assumed the indebtedness which he did not succeed completely in discharging before 1848.

On May 7, 1833, Lincoln was appointed postmaster at New Salem. The business of the office amounted to little and his return therefrom was trifling, but there was a notion that the post office brought customers into the store. So long as Lincoln remained in partnership with Berry the post office was conducted in the Lincoln & Berry store. When Lincoln withdrew he became a clerk in the Samuel Hill store, one door west, and carried his office with him. There was not much to carry, however, as it is currently reported that he carried the letters about in his hat. We know that later he had a habit of carrying manuscripts in the "stove pipe" headgear he wore in those days.

The Lincoln & Berry store, now in part restored, was a one-story frame building consisting of two rooms, the large store room proper in front and a small "lean-to" or "shed" room at the rear. The latter was apparently used as a sleeping room and for the storage of surplus stock. The Lincoln League found parts of the original foundation intact when restoring the structure. The corners were in place, thus establishing that the main building was twenty feet square on the outside. Lincoln and Berry did not own the building but, like Radford, rented it from William Green. This structure, like all the stores of New Salem, had a porch at the front. This unfortunately has *not* been restored.

Just west of the Lincoln & Berry store was the Hill & McNeil store, the first established in the village. Hill's partner was John McNamar, who came to the place under the assumed name of McNeil and at one time was engaged to be married to Ann Rutledge. Ann's brother Robert prepared for Herndon in 1866 a manuscript containing this story: "In 1830, my sister being but seventeen years of age, a stranger, calling himself John McNeil, came to New Salem. He boarded with Mr. Cameron and was keeping a store with Samuel Hill. A friendship grew up between McNeil and Ann, which resulted in an engagement to marry. . . . It seems that his father had failed in business and the son . . . had determined to make a fortune, pay off his father's debts, and return him to his former social and financial standing. With this view, he left his home secretly in order to avoid pursuit by his parents, and changed his name. . . . He prospered in business—and, pending his engagement to Ann—he revealed his true name, returned to Ohio to relieve his parents from their embarrassment and to bring the family with him to Illinois. On his return to Ohio, several years having elapsed, he found his father in declining health, and perhaps the circumstances of the family prevented his return. . . . At all events, he was absent two or three years." He did not write and Ann, after cherishing her affection for him for a time, forgot, and gave her heart to Abraham Lincoln. When McNamar returned to New Salem in the autumn of 1835 Ann Rutledge was dead. Little basis had he for the claim made to Herndon that she "died for love of him" and that she never loved Lincoln. Moreover, his treatment of her mother and family after the death of Ann and her father is scarcely reconcilable with his story of *his* regard for her. In fact he was not able to point out to Herndon the site of her grave in the Concord Cemetery or for that matter the grave of his own mother. He seems to have been a bold, calculating, practical, unemotional, tight-fisted fellow.

Samuel Hill, who continued the business after the departure of "McNeil," was postmaster from the establishment of the office in December, 1829, until November, 1831. He was succeeded by Isaac P. Chrisman but, upon the failure of Chrisman Brothers, was reappointed. He held the office until May 7, 1833, when Abraham Lincoln was appointed. Lincoln was postmaster until 1836 when the office was discontinued.

Hill built a two story residence just west of his grocery. This was the most pretentious house in the village and, after the removal of Hill to Petersburg in 1839, it served as a hotel and was known as Hill's Tavern. Today only a depression marks the site of the house The store building was removed by Hill to Petersburg and in it he conducted a store.

Just across from the Hill residence was the office and residence of Dr. John Allen, who came to the town in 1830, living here until his removal to Petersburg about 1838. He was a temperance advocate and organized a temperance society in the village. He was a friend of Lincoln and ministered to his health when that was necessary. Lincoln afterward served as Allen's attorney in a case against Hill tried at Petersburg. The Allen house was a three room structure but the small log enclosure now standing gives no idea of its character.

The only other structure that stands in the village is Henry Onstott's cooper shop at the extreme west end of Main Street. Onstott, a native of Kentucky, came to New Salem in 1830. At first he lived and operated a cooper shop in the east end of the village. In 1833 he moved into the Rutledge Inn, just vacated by James Rutledge, who had removed to a farm on Sand Ridge. He operated the Inn for two years, during

which time Lincoln was a patron, in the meantime
building a larger residence and a more commodious shop
at the west end of the street. These structures
he occupied from 1835 to 1840 when he removed
them to Petersburg. The cooper shop was weather-
boarded; a wing was added to it and for many years
it served as a dwelling. It was purchased by the
Lincoln League in 1922, restored to its former condition
and re-erected on its original site. This shop was
completed about a year before Onstott built his residence and it was before the fireplace of this building that
Lincoln studied surveying while Isaac Onstott, the son
of the owner, fed shavings to the fire to make the light
by which Lincoln read.

The League has placed markers at other spots
showing the locations of the various houses and shops.
Across Green's Rocky Branch to the south of the
village was the school presided over by Mentor Graham,
who taught Lincoln grammar, and not far away was
the village cemetery. It is said that when Lincoln was
studying surveying he often came to Graham's house
for help and together they worked over the problems
until late at night.

Reep relates that a barbecue-pit was formed just
north of the Hill store and that "the gander pulling
contests were *pulled* off on the ridge, south of Offut's
store where the little grove now stands. The horse
races occurred on west Main Street, . . . starting or
ending near the Berry and Lincoln store." In the old
days the road to Springfield ran south from Main
Street, west of the Rutledge Inn. Its course can still
be traced leading down the hillside to Green's Rocky
Branch.

The visitor at New Salem will want to drive into
Petersburg and to Oaklawn Cemetery to visit the
grave of Ann Rutledge, with whose name that of
Lincoln has in recent years often been associated.
That Lincoln loved Ann Rutledge I think has been

THE RUTLEDGE TAVERN
Old Salem State Park, near Petersburg, Illinois

HENRY ONSTOTT'S COOPER SHOP
Old Salem State Park

Photographs by the Author

established, and that her early death should have
deeply affected him is not to be wondered at, but that
she was the only woman he ever loved or that her
death seriously affected his subsequent married life is
undoubtedly the fabrication of imaginative and senti-
mental writers.   Lincoln by the time he knew the
sweet-faced Ann had seen enough of life to be somewhat sobered by it.   He had also learned that all one
can do in the face of circumstance is to carry on and
have faith, and that abiding faith Mr. Lincoln often
expressed by word and deed.

The Rutledges remained in New Salem until 1834
when their fortunes became so involved that they were
compelled to remove from the town.   They had already sold their farm on Sand Ridge, as had the Camer-
ons.   The Cameron house on Sand Ridge was however
unoccupied and into this both families moved.   These
were hard days for the family, and those of the children
who could do so were forced to "work out" among
the neighbors.   Ann for a time worked at the home of
Uncle Jimmie Short and here Lincoln is said to have
wooed her.   It was at this time that Uncle Jimmie
became acquainted with Lincoln, and later, when the
young surveyor's instruments and horse were sold to
satisfy a debt that Lincoln owed to a Mr. Van Bergen,
Short redeemed the property and returned it to Abe.

While the Rutledges were in straightened circumstances in 1835, the son David managed to stay in
school at Illinois College in Jacksonville and Dr.
Barton introduces a letter* written by David to his
father in which he included a postscript to Ann in-
dicating her intention of entering the Female Academy
in Jacksonville.   He addresses her as "Valued Sister"
and says "I am glad to hear that you have a notion of
coming to school, and I earnestly recommend to you
that you would spare no time from improving your
education and mind.   Remember that time is worth

* Barton, Trans. Ill. State Hist. Soc. for 1926, 120.

more than all gold therefore throw away none of your golden moments. . . ."

Barton believes that Lincoln, too, planned to go to Jacksonville to school, but of this we have no sure proof. Whatever the plans of the pair were, they were short-lived, for at the very time this letter was received Ann was already ill with malarial fever, of which she died after an illness of six weeks. Lincoln is said to have visited her once during this period "riding over from New Salem" where he was postmaster, surveyor and a representative from Sangamon County. She died August 25, 1835, in the Cameron cabin on Sand Ridge, which at the time was owned by the same John McNamar who had wooed her but left her forgotten in 1833.

Ann was buried in old Concord Cemetery on the McGrady Rutledge farm which is about a mile from the present Concord Church. Here also stood the original Concord Church and in this cemetery were buried the Rutledges, the Armstrongs, the Berrys and other early settlers of Sand Ridge. The place is now given over to undergrowth but is identified by the tombstones, many of which are in place and legible. Ann's father, who died shortly after his daughter, lies buried here, as does the body of her brother David, who died in 1842. The burying ground, well fenced, is a quiet and peaceful God's acre.

But Ann was not destined to lie unmolested under wild flower and sod, for in 1890 the promoters of Oakland Cemetery in Petersburg, believing that some advertising value might accrue from the fact that Ann's remains lay buried in their plot, sought permission of Ann's cousin, McGrady Rutledge, to remove the body to Oakland. To this he agreed, and in May of that year her remains were transferred to the new cemetery which, endowed with certain natural beauty, has been improved with the passing of the years. Especially handsome was the place in late October of

THE GRAVE OF ANN RUTLEDGE
Oaklawn Cemetery, Petersburg, Illinois
Photograph by the Author

last year when the ground was carpeted with russet leaves and the very light of the sun was tinted a deep amber as it filtered through the golden leafed maple trees.

For a number of years the simple headstone inscribed with her name did duty as a marker at Ann's grave, but in January, 1921, a large block of dark grey Quincy granite was set in place upon the spot. The movement so to mark the place was largely inspired by the late Henry B. Rankin of Springfield, and was participated in by a number of Menard County people. Mr. Rankin as a youth was a law student in the office of Lincoln and Herndon.

The following verse, taken from Edgar Lee Masters' poem "Ann Rutledge" and published in the "Spoon River Anthology" is inscribed on the face of the block:

OUT OF ME, UNWORTHY AND UNKNOWN,
THE VIBRATIONS OF DEATHLESS MUSIC;
"WITH MALICE TOWARD NONE, WITH CHARITY FOR ALL,"
OUT OF ME, FORGIVENESS OF MILLIONS TOWARD MILLIONS,
AND THE BENEFICENT FACE OF A NATION
SHINING WITH JUSTICE AND TRUTH.
I AM ANN RUTLEDGE WHO SLEEPS BENEATH THESE WEEDS,
BELOVED OF ABRAHAM LINCOLN,
WEDDED TO HIM, NOT THROUGH UNION
BUT THROUGH SEPARATION.
BLOOM FOREVER, O REPUBLIC,
FROM THE DUST OF MY BOSOM!

Below are her dates: January 7th, 1813—August 25th, 1835.

CHAPTER VIII

THE SCENES OF LINCOLN'S BLACK HAWK WAR SERVICE

IN THE spring of 1832, shortly after Abraham Lincoln had published his hand-bill announcing for the first time his candidacy for the Illinois Legislature, a messenger rode into New Salem posting and scattering about the stores another hand-bill. This latter paper bore a proclamation from Governor Reynolds calling the militia of the section to a rendezvous at Beardstown on April 22, to put down an uprising of the Sac Indians under Chief Black Hawk.

Upon reading the Governor's proclamation, Lincoln took a piece of paper, wrote out an agreement to volunteer for the service and signed his name, inviting others to join with him in raising a company. In the meantime, so it seems, James O. Kirkpatrick, the owner of the sawmill at Sangamo Town, was raising a similar company. When it was learned that two parties were being formed, a meeting of the volunteers at Richland, a few miles away, was arranged. Here they met, drew up a temporary muster-roll, and elected tentative officers. Kirkpatrick was ambitious to become the captain of the company, but the Clary's Grove boys, knowing that Lincoln had had an altercation with the mill-owner at the time he was constructing the flatboat for Offut, "determined to rebuke" Kirkpatrick for what they considered a "dirty trick" and put forth their friend and idol, Abraham Lincoln, as their leader. Jack Armstrong was made first sergeant.

As every reader knows, the Black Hawk War was not a prolonged struggle but rather a futile attempt of a few Indians to regain the lands they had once owned in the Rock River country of Illinois. Lincoln's election to captaincy was confirmed at Beardstown on April 29 and his company was included in the Fourth Regiment, mounted volunteers, of General Samuel Whiteside's brigade.

The brigade went from Beardstown to Oquawka on the Mississippi, where they were to receive supplies sent down by boat from Fort Armstrong (Rock Island). They then followed the old Indian trail to a point near the mouth of the Rock River just south of the present city of Rock Island. Here they arrived on May 7 and were formally inducted into the service of the United States by General Henry Atkinson. The site of their encampment, known today as Lincoln Camp, is just west of the corporation-limits of the town of Milan, which lies on the south bank of the Rock and opposite Black Hawk's village, Sauk-E-Nuk.

From Rock Island they moved up the Rock River to Dixon's Ferry, burning the Prophet's village (Prophetstown) en route, and thence to the scene of Stillman's battle and defeat on Sycamore Creek in Ogle County (May 15). Here Lincoln saw some dead Indians, the only Indians he saw during the "war." From this point he marched via Dixon southeastward to Ottawa, and at Ottawa his company was mustered out (May 27).

Two days later he re-enlisted as a mounted ranger under Captain Elijah Iles. This body made a march to Galena on the Mississippi, a distance of about a hundred and twenty-five miles, and returned. On June 16 this company was mustered out and Lincoln again enlisted in Captain Jacob M. Earley's company (June 20). This party moved to Dixon, then to Kellogg's Grove and back to Dixon. At Kellogg's Grove (June 25) where the party arrived shortly after a skirmish, Lincoln helped to bury the five men who had been killed by the Indians. From Dixon the detachment went north to Turtle Village (Beloit, Wisconsin) then to Whitewater, where Lincoln was mustered out (July 11).

On the night before he was discharged Lincoln's horse was stolen and he was compelled to walk to Dixon and then to Peoria. At Peoria he and John T. Stuart of Springfield secured a canoe and together floated and paddled down the Illinois to Havana. From Havana they walked overland to their respective homes. Lincoln arrived just in time (late July) to re-enter the race for the State Assembly against the Rev. Peter Cartwright. I think no one attributes much in Lincoln's life to the influence of this experience. He considered it largely as a lark and in later years often made sport of his "war time" service.

The territory through which Captain Abraham Lincoln's company marched during the Black Hawk War is one of the most picturesque in the Illinois country. Several of the important present-day state highways cross the twelve counties through which his route passed, and several of the towns like Rock Island, Beardstown, Dixon, and Ottawa have deep historic interest for the tourist.

Beardstown on the Illinois River is a typical river town laid out in 1827. It has many Lincoln associations and the residents point out the old court house where in 1854 Lincoln won the famous "Armstrong murder case." This structure is now used as the city hall. During the Black Hawk War the city served as the base of supplies for the Illinois troops, and northward over the old stage road of that day Captain Lincoln marched his raw recruits toward the scene of action. Illinois State Road No. 3, via Rushville, Macomb, and Monmouth, approximates the old stage route that in Lincoln's time ran northward from Beardstown, then an important river port.

Few perhaps realize the antiquity of Rock Island. The present city is modern in every respect. Its prox-

imity to the island in the river, which gives it its name,
and to the Rock River which meets the "father of
waters" just below its corporation limits, has made it
an important geographical situation to white man and
Indian alike. In its southern portion is the salient
headland known in history as Black Hawk's Watch
Tower, and not far away are evidences of occupation
by the Mound Builders. In the early part of the
seventeenth century this country was the hunting
ground of the Illini (Illinois Indians). About 1680 the
Sacs and Foxes, driven from their home on the Saint
Lawrence, migrated to northern Illinois and in 1722
came to the mouth of Rock River. The Sacs settled
at Sauk-E-Nuk (Sac Village) and the Foxes not far
away. Sauk-E-Nuk was the home of the Sacs until it
was destroyed during the Black Hawk War. Here they
had dwelt continuously for 109 years. The population
is reputed to have varied from three thousand to
eleven thousand souls and the village is said to have
been "laid out with streets and squares like a modern
city." The surrounding terrain is as picturesque as
any in the whole western country. "No wonder,"
remarks J. C. Cummings, "the Sacs loved Sauk-E-
Nuk."*

During the Revolution the Illinois country was
disputed territory. At the beginning of the war Illinois
belonged to England, but Virginia was determined
to take it and Governor Patrick Henry sent Colonel
George Rogers Clark to accomplish this purpose.
Clark was instructed to do two things: "protect the
settlers in Kentucky," and "take Indiana and Illinois."
Clark captured Kaskaskia on the Mississippi and then
proceeded to Vincennes on the Wabash. By October,
1778 the military occupation was complete.

The British, however, determined to recover the
Illinois territory and dispatched several expeditions
to accomplish this purpose. These failed, due to

* Journal Ill. Hist. Soc., April, 1927, 50.

several causes, although a British Indian force, which descended the Mississippi and attacked the towns near the present Saint Louis, made a considerable inroad into the scant population of the district, killing sixty at the Battle of Pancour (St. Louis), May 26, 1780. On May 27, they crossed the river and attacked Cahokia in Illinois but, failing to take the place, they retreated northward.

Colonel John Montgomery, who came to Illinois with Clark, pursued the force northward with 350 men, among them 100 Spaniards from Pancour and 100 French from Cahokia. Clark gave Montgomery orders to follow the Illinois to the site of Ft. Creve Coeur (Peoria), then cross the state and attack the Sac and Fox villages on the Rock River. He left Cahokia on June 4, returning by July 28, in the meantime burning Sauk-E-Nuk, although opposed by a force of 700 Indians. Thus the struggle at Sauk-E-Nuk became the "westernmost battle of the Revolution."

The visitor to Rock Island will see in the southern part of that city a marker unveiled on July 16, 1926, by the Colonel John Montgomery Chapter of the Sons of the American Revolution. It bears the following inscription:

SITE OF SAUK-E-NUK
SAC VILLAGE BURNED BY COLONEL JOHN MONTGOMERY
JULY, 1780,
WESTERNMOST BATTLE OF THE REVOLUTION
Marked July 16, 1926, by the Colonel John Montgomery Chapter of the Sons of the American Revolution.

On June 29, 1927, Governor Small of Illinois affixed his signature to a bill constituting Black Hawk's Watch Tower a State Park. Thus this portion of old Sauk-E-Nuk, the village where Black Hawk was born, is perpetually preserved to the public. The new park consists of some 175 acres, adjoining the city of Rock Island. It has a front of a half mile on the Rock River,

one of the most picturesque streams in the Middle
West. The tract is wooded, has never been touched
by the plow and gradually rises to the point or bluff,
known as the "Tower," which stands 150 feet above
the river.

From this "Tower" one may look across the valley
of the Rock, upstream for several miles, or in the
opposite direction to the bluffs on the west bank of the
Mississippi three miles away. The river at this point
is a portion of the Illinois-Michigan canal connecting
Lake Michigan and the Mississippi and therefore
affords deep water boating. From the "Tower" one
may look across Vandruff's Island to Milan, and to the
place where in 1832 Captain Abraham Lincoln's company camped and where he was sworn into the service.
Just below the bluff were the "rapids" over which the
"regulars" had such difficulty in getting their barges
of army supplies when they pushed up Rock River in
pursuit of Black Hawk.

An excursion up the valley of the Rock River by
way of Prophetstown and Sterling to Dixon is a
pleasant journey. Prophetstown is the site of the old
Indian village of Wabokreskick ("White Cloud"), the
mixed Sac and Winnebago Indian "prophet" who, in
the thirties, exercised considerable influence over the
western Indians. It was he who assured Black Hawk
that, if the Sacs determined to regain their lands in
Illinois, they might expect to receive help from the
Ottawas, Winnebagos and other tribes, as well as from
the British.

When Black Hawk heard this he decided to make
the start that brought on the Black Hawk War. Many
of the Indians, however, on the advice of Chief Keokuk
refused to aid in his enterprise, but, in spite of this,
Black Hawk in April, 1832, returned to the mouth of
the Rock River and proceeded to the Winnebago
country via Prophetstown. General Atkinson, stationed at Fort Armstrong, ordered the Indians to

return home across the Mississippi, but Black Hawk paid no attention. At Prophetstown he found that the Winnebagos were not disposed to enter a war against the white man but he pressed on, engaging a force of volunteers under Major Stillman in a skirmish in the eastern part of Ogle County on May 14. It was at this spot that Abraham Lincoln's company, as part of the force dispatched from Rock Island, arrived on May 15. Eleven white men and four or five Indians were killed.

An interesting historic fact is the service in this area of Jefferson Davis, later Secretary of War and president of the ill-fated Confederacy. In 1829 Davis, a young West Point graduate, was stationed at Ft. Winnebago, then under construction on the Fox-Wisconsin River portage. Here he had charge of obtaining timbers and other matters of construction. He remained at this point until 1831 when he was transferred to Ft. Crawford at the mouth of the Wisconsin River. In the autumn of 1831 he was dispatched by Colonel Zachary Taylor to dislodge some white squatters who had taken up residence on the Indians' lands at Dubuque, Iowa. In the spring of 1832 he had proposed a visit to his home in Mississippi but the Black Hawk troubles detained him. Davis served as adjutant to Colonel Taylor, and with the "regulars" pushed up Rock River reaching Dixon about the middle of May.

Apparently Davis made the trip to Galena participated in by Lincoln, returning to Dixon as did Lincoln and then marching north on June 27, as also did Lincoln, now a member of Earley's company. Presumably Lincoln learned who Davis was, but he was *not* sworn into service by the young West Pointer as has often been asserted.

Lincoln did not stay until the completion of the war, as we have seen. The end of that struggle came with the defeat of the Indians at the Battle of Bad

Axe (Wisconsin), August 2. Lincoln by that time was back in New Salem with his hat in the political ring against Peter Cartwright. Four days later he was beaten at the polls, this "the only time," as he later said, that he "was defeated on the direct vote of the people."

Dixon's Ferry on the Rock River was an important point during the Black Hawk War. It had long been known and was for years counted by the Indians an easy place to cross the Rock, a stream known to them as the Sinnissippi. The opening of the lead mines at Galena on the Mississippi made necessary a ferry at this point. The site of the ferry was at the foot of Hennepin Avenue in Dixon, the present seat of Lee County. John Dixon began the operation of the ferry in 1828.

"When," says a recent writer, "the promoters of the Lincoln Highway (Illinois Route No. 6) routed the trail across the continent through Dixon perhaps they planned better than they knew. By accident more than design they brought it to touch the very site of the block house where Abraham Lincoln served in the Black Hawk War in 1832." The block house is not famous only because of Lincoln's association with it. Here too served Zachary Taylor, later also to become President, and Jefferson Davis, whose name in after years was much to be associated with the movement Lincoln sought to defeat. Other important men here at the time were Governor John Reynolds of Illinois, General Atkinson and Lieutenant Robert Anderson, later the defender of Fort Sumter. There is a story that Lincoln is said to have asked Anderson when the latter reported to him at the White House, "Major, do you remember ever having met me before?" The Major is said to have answered, "No, Mr. President." "Well my memory is better than yours," said Mr. Lincoln, "You mustered me into the service of the United States in 1832 in the Black Hawk

War:" It was at Dixon that Lincoln had seen him. In 1921 the State of Illinois acquired the title to the ground where stood the old block house, thus preserving for all time this spot important in the history of the State.

While in the vicinity one will want to drive on to Oregon (18 miles) and the Black Hawk Monument. This splendid statue, executed by Lorado Taft, stands sixty feet high and is constructed of reinforced concrete. It represents the chief with folded arms, in contemplative mood, gazing for miles across the valley of the Rock River, for over a century the "happy hunting ground" of his people. Lincoln and his company marched this way in going to Stillman Valley in May, 1832.

The highway (Route No. 2) is on the west side of the river and above Oregon a splendid view of the monument can be had from the road. But there are those who will want to visit it. This is done by crossing the river at Oregon and taking a road past the fair grounds northward for about a mile to the monument. The road is *not* paved, but is in good condition during most of the year. Just below Oregon on the east side of the river is the picturesque estate of Ex-governor Lowden of Illinois, known as Sinnissippi Farm. Above Oregon on the west side of the river is the estate of the late Senator Medill McCormick, one of the show places of the section. In the court-house yard in the town is Lorado Taft's simple but beautiful sculptural tribute to the veterans of the Civil War.

From Oregon one may take a picturesque and scenic drive (Route No. 2) northward (26 miles) to the thriving city of Rockford, the home of that splendid women's school, Rockford College, or via Mendota (Route No. 2) to Ottawa (Route No. 7). At Utica one may turn right, cross the broad stream of the Illinois River, and drive directly into Starved Rock State Park, one of the historic and scenic spots of the Illinois country,

BLACK HAWK MONUMENT, NEAR OREGON, ILLINOIS
By Courtesy of Portland Cement Association

the scene of the last stand of the Illini, the site of old
St. Louis, established by La Salle in 1682, and the site
of the first mission in Illinois, founded by Father
Marquette. This historic place, annually visited by
thousands, comprises some nine hundred acres of
wooded bluffs and valley land and lies along the south
bank of the Illinois River. It is admittedly one of the
most beautiful spots between the Allegheny and
Rocky Mountains.

Six miles east of the Park lies Ottawa, the scene of
one episode in Lincoln's Black Hawk War experience,
and on August 21, 1858, the theatre of one of the great
forensic encounters between Mr. Lincoln and Stephen
A. Douglas. Route No. 7 leads eastward via Joliet to
Chicago. If one desires to go south he may take
Route No. 23 to Streator and go west over Route 17
to Route 2, which leads southward to Bloomington
and the heart of the Lincoln Country.

CHAPTER IX

OLD VANDALIA—LINCOLN'S FIRST POLITICAL SERVICE

WE HAVE recounted Lincoln's unsuccessful race for the legislature in the late summer of 1832. Two years later he announced himself as a candidate, this season having more time to devote to his canvass of the territory. In 1832 he had only returned from the Black Hawk War and had little better than a month in which to make a canvass. This year he had most of the summer, for he had little else to do. Moreover, he had in the meantime been appointed postmaster at New Salem and deputy surveyor of Sangamon County. These official recognitions of his abilities cannot but have helped his standing in the community and his continued residence and work about the county for the past two years enabled him to widen his circle of acquaintances. This circle had now become so broad that Lincoln often spoke of his canvass of '34 as a "sort of handshaking campaign."

Sangamon County was entitled to four representatives in the State Assembly, and among those elected Lincoln stood second in popularity, polling 1376 votes; this in face of the fact that he ran as a Whig candidate in a predominantly Democratic district. The debts incurred through his business venture with Berry and the legal difficulties that arose therefrom had so stripped Lincoln of ready cash that he had to borrow two hundred dollars from a friend to get himself started in his new career as a lawmaker. However, he purchased a new suit of clothes, took the stage for Vandalia, the capital, and arrived there looking as prosperous and

well attired as most of the newly elected members of
the Ninth General Assembly.

Vandalia, the capital of that day, is one of the
oldest towns in the State of Illinois. By the first state
constitution Kaskaskia on the Mississippi was made
the capital. This was back in 1809 when Illinois was
separated from Indiana. This constitution further
provided that the General Assembly should "petition
Congress for a grant to the State of four sections of
land for a seat of the government." Congress granted
the land March 3, 1819, and the capital commission
immediately set about to lay out a town, sell lots and
construct a temporary capitol. The official records were
transferred from Kaskaskia in December, 1820, and
Vandalia became the seat of government.

A "public" or "capitol square" three hundred and
twenty feet square was laid out and here the first
"Capitol," a small frame structure, was erected. This
building was burned in 1823 but another structure was
at once built. This remained in use until 1836 when
it was replaced by the two-story brick structure that
today stands as a state monument but which since 1839
has served as the court house of Fayette County. The
structure was built by the citizens of Vandalia when,
during Lincoln's term as an assemblyman, the agitation to remove the capital to Springfield arose. In
spite of the erection of the building, then considered
a fine public edifice, the legislature selected Springfield
as the seat of government in 1837.

In the old days before the northern section of the
state was so thickly settled, Vandalia was near the
center of population. It was, moreover, the terminus
of the National Road just constructed and on a direct
line between Terre Haute and Saint Louis, the eventual
terminus. The old Vandalia Railroad, now of the
Pennsylvania System, was laid out parallel to the old
National Road. When Lincoln came to Vandalia as a
legislator, the town was still small, having a population

of about eight hundred. But its population was not a measure of its importance, and, as capital of the state, it attained a certain dignity and renown because of the important personalities who associated here. More-over, there were no large towns in the state at the time. The City by the Lake (Chicago) was granted her first village charter at Vandalia in 1832.

While Vandalia of that day was not much of a town, it boasted two church buildings, a Methodist and a Presbyterian, several hostelries and two newspapers. Like all towns in the state at the time, it was deep in mud in the winter time and dusty in the summer. The new capitol building had not as yet been built when Lincoln first took his seat and the Assembly was meet-ing in the Methodist church. Already the matter of the removal of the capital was an important question, but the "log-rolling" that accomplished this purpose was not to take place until the next session. Lincoln with John Dawson, William Carpenter, and John T. Stuart (later to become Mr. Lincoln's law-partner) represented Sangamon in the Ninth General Assembly but, although he creditably held his position, Lincoln did not make a name for himself at either the regular or the extra session called in December, 1835. He was appointed to the Committee on Public Accounts and Expenditures and at this session met for the first time his future political adversary, Stephen A. Douglas.

By 1836 a new apportionment had been made which resulted in sending to the Assembly nine men from Sangamon County. This delegation, the largest from any county in the state, consisted of two senators, Archer G. Herndon and Job Fletcher, and seven repre-sentatives, Abraham Lincoln, William F. Elkin, Ninian W. Edwards, John Dawson, Daniel Stone, Robert L. Wilson, and Andrew McCormick. It is interesting to note that Lincoln polled the largest vote of any of these men (1716) and that the combined heights of these gentlemen equaled fifty-four feet. For this reason they were called the "Long Nine."

The Sangamon delegation went to Vandalia for the Tenth General Assembly with the avowed purpose of removing the capital to Springfield and were prepared to "swap" votes with other "interests" to attain their end. As a result of the "log-rolling," Springfield emerged the capital city in spite of the fact that Vandalia had made a serious bid for consideration by erecting a commodious building to house the state government.* One incident connected with this session was the retreat of Mr. Lincoln and Joseph Gillespie through a window of the room in which the Assembly was meeting in order to break a quorum. Such tactics led to the popular attribution of bad legislation or the defeat of desired measures to the activities of the "Long Nine."

Lincoln's association with Vandalia was not to be lengthy but it was long enough for him to enter into a considerable part of the legislation of the day which looked forward to the internal improvement of the state, a subject very close to his heart. Railroads, canals and all sorts of internal improvement schemes received attention and appropriation, a cool $50,000, a large sum in those days, being voted for the improvement of the Kaskaskia River, a negligible stream in which, as the story goes, one indignant assemblyman said "turtles were wont to go aground." But these optimistic improvement schemes were soon transferred to Springfield, for in 1839 the offices of the state were moved to that city, the property being transported thither by wagon. At this time the capitol building was donated by the state to Fayette County and it became the court house of that county.

As the first important seat of government in Illinois and the first scene of Lincoln's political life, Vandalia

* Jacksonville, Peoria, Alton, and Illiopolis were other towns seeking the location of the capital.

is interesting and many people touring the Lincoln Country go there. It is easily reached by one coming from the Indiana Lincoln Country. One should leave Illinois State Route No. 1 at Marshall, turning left on Illinois State Route No. 11 which closely follows the old National Road of Lincoln's time. From Vandalia one may go via Route No. 2 to Decatur, the first town in Illinois connected with Lincoln's life, or via Pana and Taylorville (Route 24 at Pana) directly to Springfield (78 miles). Vandalia is reached from Saint Louis via Route No. 11 (69 miles).

The most important spot connected with Lincoln's life at Vandalia is, of course, the old Capitol, long the Fayette County court house, but now the property of the State. This simple Greek Revival building is in a good state of preservation and is as originally constructed with the exception that the large brick columns that supported the north and south porticoes have been (1899) replaced by ugly iron columns and balconies. Let us hope that the State Department of Public Works and Buildings will restore these one-time handsome features of the structure.

The interior of the edifice is well preserved. On the lower floor a broad hall sixteen feet wide runs through from portico to portico; a narrower hall nine feet wide passing through the building from east to west, thus dividing the lower story into four large rooms. A massive staircase leads from the lower hall to the upper story. At the head of this stairway one turns west into the House of Representatives, preserved intact, where Lincoln and the "Long Nine" sat. The walls of the structure are of brick; the roof of standing-seam metal. A pretty cupola crowns the intersecting ridges of the porticoes and main roof.

THE OLD CAPITOL, VANDALIA, ILLINOIS
Photograph by T. E. O'Donnell

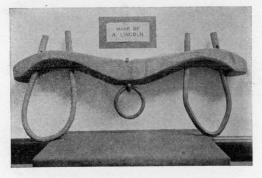

OX-YOKE MADE BY ABRAHAM LINCOLN
Property of University of Illinois, Urbana

CHAPTER X

The Springfield of Lincoln's Early Residence

WHEN Lincoln returned from the winter session of the Assembly at Vandalia (1836–7), he found New Salem on the wane. Petersburg, a new town, two miles northward, was beginning to flourish and the hope of permanence that New Salemites entertained for their place had vanished with the discontinuance of the post office.

With the establishment of the capital at Springfield that town promised to become a place of some importance and Mr. Lincoln believed that his future lay at the seat of state government. He had, moreover, just procured his license to practise law (September 9, 1836), and his old Black Hawk War comrade, John T. Stuart, had offered to take him in as a partner. Thus in March, 1837, Lincoln collected his few belongings and upon a borrowed horse rode to Springfield.

Springfield was at the time a typical, raw, western town of fewer than two thousand inhabitants. Like all middle-western towns of the day, it was laid out around a public square with the same checker-board precision that characterized Philadelphia. The streets were unpaved and in bad weather the wagons mired hub deep in the sticky black muck. Around the public square straggled "rows" of two-storied buildings, the lower floors of which contained the shops of the town, the upper stories the offices of professional men or living quarters for the store-keepers' families.

The story of Lincoln's arrival in the capital has often been told but the account of Joshua Speed is perhaps the most trustworthy. "He had ridden into town on a borrowed horse," says Speed, "with no earthly property save a pair of saddle-bags containing a few clothes. I was a merchant at Springfield, and kept a large country store. . . . Lincoln came into the store with the saddle-bags on his arm. He said he wanted to buy the furniture for a single bed." This Speed figured would cost seventeen dollars, "but small as the price was," Lincoln "was unable to pay it." "But," continues Speed, "if I would credit him till Christmas, and his experiment as a lawyer was a success, he would pay then; saying in the saddest tone, 'If I fail in this I do not know that I can ever pay you.'

"I said to him: 'You seem to be so much pained at contracting so small a debt, I think I can suggest a plan by which you can avoid the debt, . . . I have a large room with a double bed upstairs, which you are very welcome to share with me.' 'Where is your room?' said he. 'Upstairs,' said I, pointing to a . . . winding stairs which led . . . to my room. He took his saddle-bags, . . . went upstairs, set them on the floor, and came down with the most changed expression of countenance. Beaming with pleasure, he exclaimed: 'Well, Speed, I'm moved.'"

The Speed store no longer stands, but a bronze tablet in the east show-window of Meyer Brothers Store at southwest corner of Fifth and Washington Streets marks the site and bears this inscription:

When Abraham Lincoln arrived in Springfield in 1837 there stood on this site a two story building. The first floor was occupied by the general store of Joshua F. Speed. On the second floor one room was shared by Lincoln and Speed as a bedroom from 1837 until 1841.

For a number of years Speed's store served as headquarters for Lincoln and a congenial group including Douglas, Baker, Calhoun, Browning, Lamborn, and others who discussed all sorts of questions from politics to religion. "The store had a large fire-place in the rear," says Herndon, then a clerk in the establishment, "and around it the lights of the town collected every evening. As the sparks flew from the crackling logs, another and more brilliant fire flashed when these great minds came into collision. . . . Speed, Lincoln, Charles R. Hurst, and I slept in the room upstairs."

Lincoln had not been in Springfield long when there appeared in the *Sangamon Journal* (April 12, 1837), the following professional card, the first published by Mr. Lincoln:

> J. T. STUART AND A. LINCOLN.
> ATTORNEYS and Counsellers at Law, will practice, conjointly, in the Courts of this Judicial Circuit. Office No. 4, Hoffman's Row, upstairs.
> Springfield, april 12, 1837.

Just below this card appeared an announcement that "the partnership heretofore existing between" John T. Stuart and Henry E. Dummer had "been dissolved by common consent."

The office of the new firm, says Herndon, "was in the upper story of a building opposite the northwest corner of the present Court House Square. In the room underneath, the county court was held. The furniture was in keeping with the pretensions of the firm—a small lounge or bed, a chair containing a buffalo robe . . . , a hard wooden bench, a feeble attempt at a book case, and a table which answered for a desk. . . . At the time of Lincoln's entry into the office, Stuart was just recovering from the effects of a congressional race in which he had been loser. He was still deeply absorbed in politics," and "did not give to the law his undivided time. . . . Thus more or less responsibility in the management of business and the conduct of cases soon devolved upon Lincoln."

The building in which the future President had his first law office comes down to us, but in remodelled condition. Moreover, the name of Stuart still clings to it, and at the left of the door of the Stuart Confectionery Company (109 N. Fifth St.) one will find a tablet with this inscription:

SITE OF THE FIRST LAW OFFICE OF
A. LINCOLN
1837 – 1839

SPRINGFIELD CHAPTER
SONS OF
AMERICAN REVOLUTION.

But these first months at Springfield were up-hill months and, had it not been for such friends as William Butler who took him into his own home, boarded him, and in other ways befriended him, Lincoln's lot would have been far harder than it was. For one thing he was not sure in his own mind that he wanted to marry Mary Owens of Kentucky to whom he had paid considerable attention just before his removal from New Salem. Miss Owens' sister, Mrs. Bennett Able of New Salem, was much interested in Lincoln and hoped to "make a match" between him and Mary, but neither of the young people was sure that such a "match" would prove successful. Something of Lincoln's indecision and poverty-stricken depression is shown in a letter written to Miss Owens on May 7. Among other things he said:

"This thing of living in Springfield is rather dull business after all. . . . I am often thinking of what we said of your coming to live at Springfield. I am afraid you would not be satisfied. . . . You would have to be poor without the means of hiding your poverty. Do you believe you could bear that patiently? . . . I know I should be much happier with you than the way I am, provided I saw no signs of discontent in you. What you have said to me may have been in jest or I may have misunderstood it. If so, then let it be

STEPHENS COLLEGE,
COLUMBIA, MO.

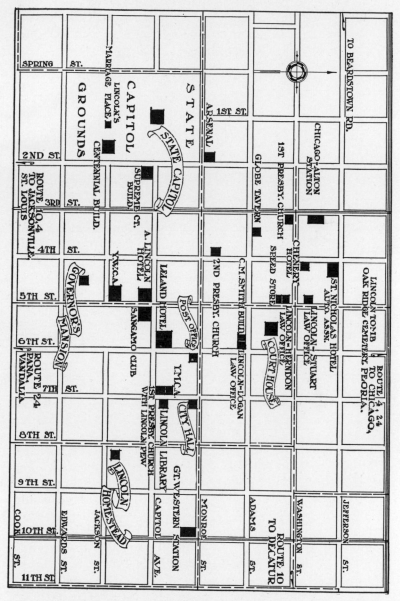

MAP OF THE LINCOLN SHRINES OF SPRINGFIELD, ILLINOIS

forgotten; if otherwise I much wish you would think seriously before you decide. For my part I have already decided. What I have said I will most positively abide by, provided you wish it. My opinion is you had better not do it. You have not been accustomed to hardship, and it may be more severe than you imagine. I know you are capable of thinking correctly on any subject; and if you deliberate maturely upon this subject before you decide, then I am willing to abide by your decision."

On August 16, after a visit to Miss Owens at New Salem, he wrote a further letter in a similar mood. I think most young women would have done as Mary Owens did. She knew that Lincoln was man enough to go through with any proposal that he had made but she wanted to be loved and loved ardently, and she was sure that she was *not*. Moreover, she did not like to have it said to her that *she could marry him*, if it would make her happy. So she did what almost every girl would have done; she declined. Returning to Kentucky, she subsequently married Jesse Vineyard and with him removed to Weston, Missouri, where she lived for many years, sending her sons to the Confederate Army when the Civil War came.

Springfield is proud of her Lincoln history and has taken great care in marking those spots hallowed through association with him. In May, 1841, Mr. Lincoln formed a partnership with Judge Stephen T. Logan, at the time one of the great lawyers of the state. The Judge is said to have had an "ability to pick out young men of potential capacity and to develop them into outstanding attorneys," but we need not attribute to him great discernment in this case for Lincoln was making for himself an increasingly larger place in the political and legal world. He had been returned to the state legislature again in 1838 and 1840, and upon many occasions had already distinguished himself as a speaker of power and a thinker of no mean caliber. This partnership lasted until 1844, when Mr. Lincoln withdrew to associate himself with Herndon in a partnership that lasted until the President's death.

The Lincoln-Logan office was located in the building directly opposite the southeast corner of the Court House Square. This structure, long known as the "old Farmers' Bank Building," is still standing. (Southwest corner of Sixth and Adams Streets.) On the Sixth Street façade of the building those interested will find a tablet with this inscription:

1841 – 1843
LOGAN AND LINCOLN
ON THE THIRD FLOOR OF THIS BUILDING
WAS LOCATED THE LAW OFFICE OF
STEPHEN T. LOGAN
AND
ABRAHAM LINCOLN

When Lincoln began his practice at Springfield the Court House was located in a group of buildings known as "Homan's Row." They were situated on the west side of Fifth Street north of Washington and were adjacent to "Hoffman's Row" where with Stuart he opened an office in 1837. Some of these buildings still stand today but, of course, very much altered.

Perhaps the building in Springfield most closely associated with the life of Lincoln, aside from his own home, was the "Old Capitol" now the Sangamon County Court House; but, when the seat of government was first transferred thither, there was as yet no capitol building, and the Assembly was forced to meet in the old Second Presbyterian Church. This edifice, no longer in existence, stood on the west side of Fourth between Monroe and Adams Streets. A tablet on the pier at the entrance of the present-day structure upon the site reads:

On this Site stood the Second Presbyterian Church, in which the First Session of the Illinois House of Representatives was held, 1839–1840, after the removal of the capital from Vandalia.

ABRAHAM LINCOLN was a member of that House of Representatives.

When the town was laid out in 1823 the public square was designated as the site of the court house. Up to 1831 a structure on the corner of Sixth and Adams Streets served as a court house but in that year a brick building was erected at the center of the square to house the county offices. This old structure, which was in 1837 demolished to make way for the state capitol, had its connection with Lincoln's life for it was here that Judge S. T. Logan entered the record of the granting of a certificate of good moral character to Lincoln as a preliminary to his admission to the bar.

When Springfield became the capital, the county commissioners conveyed the square to the State and the present interesting old Greek Revival structure was erected. This served as the state capitol until 1876 when the government was moved to the present Capitol Building. At that time the property was returned to Sangamon County. In the nineties the county business outgrew the facilities offered by the old structure; the building was raised and the present first story built under it. The building was at the same time re-roofed and the dome replaced. The edifice was completed in its present form in the spring of 1901.

Considerable information regarding the construction of the old fabric comes down to us. John F. Rague, at the time president of the Mechanics Institute of Springfield, was the architect. William Harrower was the stone contractor; James C. Sutton had the contract for the timber work and William Helmle, father of the late George H. Helmle, F. A. I. A., for many years a leading architect of the state, carved the capitals for the columns in the House of Representatives. The staircase in the rotunda was constructed by Dallman and Graham, and John E. Roll, associated with Isaac Smith and George Leggott, were the plastering contractors. John E. Roll was living at Sangamo Town when Abe Lincoln built the flatboat at that point. He kept a very complete set of books, upon the pages of which are figures covering several jobs of work which he executed for Mr. Lincoln. The structure was finally occupied by the Twelfth General Assembly, the second session of which convened on December 7, 1840. Mr. Lincoln was a member of that Assembly.

When the structure was raised in 1899, none of the original walls was changed. Thus the building above the first floor preserves the original plan. Enter the old building and you will be able to identify many of the rooms associated with Lincoln's activities. On the west side, in an office now occupied by the County Superintendent of Schools, was the State Library in the old days. Here Lincoln spent much time looking up references in connection with his work. In the northeast corner on the same floor was the suite of the State Supreme Court. Here Mr. Lincoln plead many cases and won many of his important legal victories.

The second story (present third floor) was given over to the legislative chambers and Governor's offices. The entire west side of this floor was used by the House of Representatives. This famous old hall where Lincoln sat as an Assemblyman, where he delivered his famous "house divided against itself" speech, and where his mortal remains lay in state after his assassination, is now occupied by the Circuit Court of Sangamon County. The House committee rooms were located over the north and south entrances of the building.

The Senate Chamber, occupying about half of the east side of this floor, was in the northeast corner. Committee rooms adjoined the Chamber on the south, and across the hall were the offices of the Governor and the State Superintendent of Public Instruction. It

THE OLD STATE-HOUSE
Now Sangamon County Court-House
SPRINGFIELD, ILLINOIS

Photograph by the Author

was in the Governor's office, placed at Lincoln's disposal, that he met the great stream of people who came to Springfield to see him after his election. The overflow from these crowds was accommodated in the office of Dr. Newton Bateman, then Superintendent of Public Instruction. The old Governor's office is now that of the Master-in-Chancery, the Superintendent's that of the Court Reporter.

The old rotunda with its stairway at the center was the place of many brilliant gatherings in Lincoln's time. Here took place official receptions, church fairs, revival meetings, and political gatherings. For large gatherings the speaker stood upon the landing of the stairway, thus being able to address those assembled in the rotunda on both floors. The old capitol was a noble structure in its day and indeed it is not without a certain quaint charm even in its changed form. The south portico, particularly, when seen in full sunshine, makes an attractive picture.

Other spots connected with Lincoln's earlier years at Springfield are numerous, but since few of these compare in interest with those associated with his legal successes and political victories they are often forgotten. The houses that Lincoln frequented in these years were those of William Butler, John Owsley, and Ninian W. Edwards. The Edwardses always held "open house" for the members of the legislature and doubtless Lincoln's first visit to their home was upon some such occasion. Mrs. Edwards, a Todd of Kentucky, was well known for her social graces and her entertainments, and Mr. Edwards, the son of an early governor of the State and one of the "Long Nine," was intimately known by Mr. Lincoln.

But Lincoln was presently to be attracted to the Edwards home for another reason, and that very good reason was Mary Todd of Lexington, Kentucky, the beautiful sister of Mrs. Edwards, who in 1839 came to live in Springfield. Miss Todd came of distinguished

stock on both sides of her family and had been properly
educated by Madame Mantelli and at Mrs. Ward's
Academy. Two years previously she had visited the
Illinois capital, but in 1839 she came here to reside
permanently.

We are told by Herndon that "she was a good con-
versationalist, using with equal fluency the French and
English languages. . . . She not only had a quick
intellect, but an intuitive judgment of men and their
motives." Stories are still current in the town regarding Mary Todd's entrance into Springfield society and
of the charming picture she made when she appeared
in a chic costume of "white bobinet with black velvet
sash and tie." Old ladies who a few years ago remembered her début could not recall whether or not
Abraham Lincoln was present, but it was agreed that
the socially graceful Stephen Douglas was.

Through his friendship with the Edwardses and the
influence of Joshua Speed, Lincoln was soon to become
acquainted with Miss Todd. He fell almost immediately under her spell, being "charmed with her wit and
beauty, no less than by her excellent social qualities
and profound knowledge of the strong and weak points
in individual character." Visit followed visit, Miss
Todd receiving on equal terms the quiet, sober young
lawyer and the oppositely inclined and aggressive
Douglas, who paid her "particular court." These
young men took turns in matching wits with the
brilliant girl and sitting upon the patterned haircloth
of the mahogany sofas in the Edwards parlor. Physi-
cally, perhaps, Miss Todd would have been a better
match for Mr. Douglas, but at the end of a year Mr.
Lincoln came off victor in the game and his engagement
to Miss Todd was a generally accepted fact.

But "the course of true love never did run smooth"
and there were periods of estrangement. Herndon
carries a story that the young couple were to have been
married on the first day of January, 1841, and elaborates

upon it as follows: "Careful preparations for the happy occasion were made at the Edwards mansion. The house underwent the customary renovation; the furniture was properly arranged, the rooms neatly decorated, the supper prepared and the guests invited. The latter assembled . . . and awaited in expectant pleasure the interesting ceremony. . . . The bride, bedecked in veil and silken gown, and nervously toying with the flowers in her hair, sat in the adjoining room. Nothing was lacking but the groom. For some strange reason he had been delayed. An hour passed, and the guests as well as the bride were becoming restless. But they were all doomed to disappointment. Another hour passed; messengers were sent out over town, and each returning with the same report, it became apparent that Lincoln . . . had purposely failed to appear! The bride, in grief, disappeared to her room; the wedding supper was left untouched; the guests quietly and wonderingly withdrew; the lights in the Edwards mansion were blown out, and darkness settled over all for the night. . . . By daybreak, after persistent search, Lincoln's friends found him. Restless, gloomy, miserable, desperate, he seemed an object of pity. His friends . . . fearing a tragic termination watched him closely . . . day and night. . . . Mrs. Edwards did not hesitate to regard him as insane, and of course her sister Mary shared in that view."

But, in spite of Herndon's vivid and detailed description of this unfortunate event there now seems little likelihood that it ever occurred. The papers of the day could scarcely have failed to make notice of the approaching marriage of young people so prominent, but no such notice is to be found in the existent copies of the local papers. Moreover, the records of Sangamon County reveal the issuance of no license to the contracting parties, and no invitations for such an event have ever been discovered. Thus the affair as recounted by Herndon is now completely discounted by sober students.

I think no one conversant with the facts denies that there was an estrangement about this time, or that in January of 1841 Mr. Lincoln suffered an attack of despondency that for a time put him under a great mental and nervous strain. That he was, however, a "groom gone crazy as a loon," as Herndon would have us believe, is moreover unthinkable in view of Mr. Lincoln's attendance at the meetings of the State Assembly, then in session.

Miss Mary Leighton Miles* has recently made a study of the facts surrounding this period of Mr. Lincoln's life and finds that he was in attendance at the capitol continuously from Wednesday, December 30, 1840, through January 2, 1841. January 3, being Sunday, there was no session and Mr. Lincoln did not answer roll-call on Monday the fourth. He was present at every session, however, from Tuesday the fifth through Tuesday, January 12, but was absent from Wednesday the thirteenth until Thursday the twenty-first, with the exception of Tuesday the nineteenth when he was present for a half-day. From January 21, Mr. Lincoln was present at every session until the adjournment on Monday, March 1.

During January and February Lincoln was busy keeping track of his partner's (Stuart's) chances for re-election to Congress and moreover wrote Stuart regarding other matters; the post office appointment for Dr. Henry (January 20) and the choice of Bat Webb as District Attorney (February 5). On January 23 he wrote Stuart the letter so often quoted to show that he was suffering mentally, but on the same day he had taken part in the House debate regarding the financing of the Illinois-Michigan Canal. His letters of the period show that he was despondent but that he

* Journal Illinois Historical Society, April, 1927.

was "insane" can scarcely be held, much less the story of the wedding fiasco as given by Herndon.

Early in 1841 Speed disposed of his business in Springfield and returned to Kentucky. He asked Lincoln to visit him at Louisville. This visit offered an opportunity for Herndon to add a further episode to the above quoted story. He makes Speed take Lincoln to Kentucky to recuperate from his mental derangement. "The congenial association. . . , the freedom from unpleasant reminders, the company of his staunch friend, and . . . the motherly care" of his friend's mother all help, according to Herndon, and "at last the great cloud lifted and passed away."

The plain fact is that although Lincoln is said to have "gone crazy" he did not visit Kentucky until late summer. Indeed as late as July 23, 1841, Lincoln presented the oral arguments in the case of Bailey *vs.* Cromwell before the Illinois Supreme Court. Nor did he leave Springfield before election day, which fell on August 2. The poll books for that year show that on that day he voted at Poll Number One in Springfield, supporting his partner for Congress.

After the election and legal duties were out of the way he made his way to Louisville, where he visited the Speeds until the third week in September, returning to Springfield in company with Speed. Thus in view of facts now well established, Herndon's stories of the transpirations of the January previous and of his trip to Kentucky become untenable. The engagement between Miss Todd and Lincoln had been broken, but aside from the fact that Lincoln "was saddened and melancholy over an unfortunate love affair," nothing has really been proved.

CHAPTER XI

THE SPRINGFIELD OF LINCOLN'S MARRIED LIFE

WHEN Abraham Lincoln returned from Kentucky in September, 1841, he learned that he was being popularly mentioned as a possible Whig candidate for governor of Illinois. He found it necessary to take notice of the fact through his friend Simeon Francis, the editor, who, writing in the *Sangamon Journal*, says: "Mr. Lincoln's talents and services endear him to the Whig party; but we do not believe he desires the nomination. . . ."

"It is wildly improbable," says Mary Leighton Miles, "if Lincoln went away—or more unlikely still, if he were taken away—to recover from some mental derangement, that he should find such a condition awaiting his return." He came back to his work, proceeding in a perfectly normal fashion but discussing from time to time with Speed some of his misgivings about marriage. Speed, moreover, had become engaged to Miss Fanny Henning of Lexington, Kentucky, and, since he remained in Springfield until the New Year, these friends must have had much time to compare or to contrast their cases.

Speed was married in February but was constantly in correspondence with Lincoln from the time of his return home in January, 1842. Perhaps Speed's happy consummation after his own period of misgivings fortified Lincoln, but as yet his differences with Miss Todd were not mended. On March 27 he wrote to Speed saying:

"It cannot be told how it thrills me with joy to hear you say you are 'far happier than you ever expected to be.' That much I know is enough. . . . I am not going beyond the truth when I tell you that the short space it took me to read your last letter gave me more pleasure than the total sum of all I have enjoyed since that fatal first of January, 1841. Since then it seems to me I should have been entirely happy but for the never-absent idea that there is one still unhappy whom I have contributed to make so. That kills my soul. I cannot but reproach myself for even wishing to be happy while she is otherwise."

Thus it will be seen that Lincoln still cared and cared tremendously. Sensing this, perhaps, Simeon Francis conveyed the news to his wife, who, a good friend of Miss Todd, decided to effect a reconciliation. So she gave a party one evening to which she invited both. When thus they unexpectedly met in her parlor, the man, awkward and embarrassed, the girl, cool and confident, so the story goes, Mrs. Francis put them near one another with the whispered advice to "be friends again." The awkward silence broken, they did again become friends and in the ensuing months found Mrs. Francis' parlor a convenient and hospitable place in which to meet.

The summer wore on and fall approached. In September that unpleasant but comic altercation between Mr. Lincoln and State Auditor James Shields, which almost resulted in a duel between them, took place. Miss Todd was associated with Lincoln in contributing a series of letters to the *Journal* which, purporting to have been written by an old woman in "Lost Township," were really criticisms of the actions of State officials and particularly those of the State Auditor. These drew Shields' ire, but through friends the matter was settled without bloodshed. Early in November Abraham Lincoln and Mary Todd were married.

The wedding took place at the home of the bride's sister, Mrs. Ninian W. Edwards and, although it was held in one of Springfield's aristocratic homes, it was not in any sense an elaborate affair. In fact it was a

somewhat hurried event. The current story is that
Ninian Edwards met Lincoln in the street on the morning of November 4 and Lincoln told him that he and
Mary were to be married at the parsonage that night.
The wedding could not long have been anticipated as
the license was procured on the same day. Mr.
Edwards insisted that if Mary were to be married it
should be at his house. To this Lincoln apparently
assented and Edwards set out to enlist the help of his
sister-in-law, Mrs. Benjamin Edwards, in preparation
for the event.

Guests were hastily summoned, Mary borrowed
the wedding gown of a sister, and Lincoln "slicked himself up a bit" at the home of the Butlers. Mrs.
Edwards was equal to such an occasion and when the
guests arrived she was ready for them with a great
store of "goodies" neatly arranged on the side-board.
Miss Todd, attended by her bridesmaids, awaited the
groom who entered the room with James Matheney,
best man. They met at the wide be-pillared opening
between the "double parlors" and were united in
marriage by the Rev. Charles Dresser, the Episcopal
minister of whose parish Miss Todd was a communicant.

For many years this great house was to know the
Lincolns and many an event presided over by the
graceful hostess of the place found them in attendance.
It was to this same house that Mary Lincoln returned
after the assassination of the President, and here she
lived out her broken later years, dying in the house in
1882. But she lived to see the new capitol erected
next door and witnessed the removal of the offices
from the old Greek temple-like building in the public
square which had figured so prominently in the life of
her distinguished husband.

The old house, a square brick structure, stood for
many years but was pulled down to make room for the
Illinois State Centennial Building which now stands
upon the site and houses, among other things, the fine

collection of Lincolniana gathered by the Illinois State Historical Society. Every admirer of Lincoln will want to visit this splendid collection. The Library contains over three thousand volumes on Mr. Lincoln's life, while the "Lincoln Room" houses a very important and interesting display of Lincoln relics, pictures, writings and furniture. The collection is on the third floor of the building and one should enter by the east door. The hours are 8:30 A.M. to 4:30 P.M. daily, except Sundays.

As you leave the building, stroll along the terrace at the north. At the extreme west end of this terrace you will find a bronze tablet marking the location of the Edwards house. This tablet reads:

UPON THIS SITE STOOD THE HOME OF
NINIAN WIRT EDWARDS
WHERE ABRAHAM LINCOLN AND MARY TODD
WERE UNITED IN MARRIAGE NOV. 4, 1842
AND WHERE MARY TODD LINCOLN DIED
JULY 16, 1882

A few days after the marriage Lincoln wrote to his friend Speed, "We are not keeping house, but boarding at the Globe Tavern, which is very well kept by a widow lady by the name of Beck. Our room and boarding only costs us four dollars a week." The tavern was, to be sure, an unpretentious two storied house of wood set flush upon the street at what is now 315 East Adams Street, but it was comparable with the average inn of the day and furnished what was reputed to be the "best table-board" in the town.

Like many of the buildings of the time the old Globe Tavern has long since made room for modern structures. If one walks along the north side of Adams Street between Third and Fourth Streets, however, he will come upon a tablet affixed to the modern building. It reads:

On this site stood the Globe Tavern the Home of
ABRAHAM LINCOLN and his wife from the time
of their marriage on November 4, 1842, until May
2, 1844.   Here their first child was born.

Robert Todd, the first child, was born on August 1,
1843, and we may be sure that the mother found the
tavern a difficult place in which to keep a baby. The
couple soon began looking for a house and by the first
of the year had found what suited them. On January
16, 1844, Mr. Lincoln contracted with the Rev. Charles
Dresser for the purchase of the house and lot of the
latter which stood in what was then the southeastern
outskirts of the town. The purchase price was $1500
and this Lincoln made up by the payment of $1200
cash and the conveyance of a lot in the business district.
This lot is now identified as 409, 411, 413, and 415 East
Adams Street. The Lincolns did not gain possession
until the May 2 following, remaining at the Globe
until this time.

The new Lincoln home was a white story-and-a-
half house with green shutters, located on the northeast corner of Eighth and Jackson Streets. The lot had
been acquired by Dr. Dresser, a native of Connecticut
and a graduate of Brown University, in 1839 and it
was he who erected the house thereon. We know little
regarding the construction of the original building, but
we may agree with Albert S. Edwards, once custodian
of the property that: "It is a plain old-fashioned two-
story wooden house of twelve rooms. . . . The frame
work and all the floors are of oak; the laths of hickory,
split out by hand; the doors, door frames, window
frames and weather-boarding of black walnut. The
nails, sparingly used in its construction, are all hand-
made. The most noticeable feature of its construction
from the builder's point of view, is the prodigal use of
solid walnut and strict economy in the use of iron,
wooden pegs being used wherever practicable in lieu
of the customary nail."

The house has a hallway which extends from the front door to the rear and in all probability the present staircase was a part of the original house. Just when it was remodeled and raised to full two stories is not quite plain. Mr. A. L. Bowen in an address before the members of the Lincoln Centennial Association* on February 12, 1925, epitomized the matter thus: "The transformation from a story and a half cottage to a full two-story dwelling has formed the subject for many yarns. As I have said, I have not discovered the identity of the men who made over the house, nor am I confident that the date can be definitely fixed. . . . However, there are some stories about this event that appear to be composed of facts. I believe it is literally true that Lincoln and his wife discussed the improvement for some time. He demurred at the cost, holding out that he was not financially able to undertake the project. That he had a contractor figure on the work, that the contractor's estimate convinced Mrs. Lincoln that the work would be too costly, that Lincoln was away when Mrs. Lincoln sought the advice of another carpenter whose estimate was much less than the first's and that she ordered the work done, I am convinced are facts. Whether Lincoln conspired with the first contractor to deceive his wife, as some have intimated, I do not believe we can either prove or disprove."

The house was originally warmed by fireplaces, but Mr. Lincoln did not like fireplaces so he had the openings closed and installed wood stoves. It is understood that there was a wood stove in each room. The visitor today will find the house in much the same condition that it appeared in the days of the Lincolns, the arrangement on the first floor being quite obvious. The up-stairs rooms were used as follows: The front room on the second floor, north side, was Mr. Lincoln's bed room; the second room on this side was that of Mrs. Lincoln and the younger boys. The back room

* Lincoln Centennial Association Papers, 1925.

on the north side was the maid's. The front room on the south side was the guest room, the second on that side being Robert's. The present bathroom was used as a trunk room.

The Lincolns occupied this house with the exception of the time that he was in Congress (November, 1847—March, 1849) and the last few days before they departed for Washington after Mr. Lincoln's election. Here three of their children were born and from this house one of those children was buried. Here also in 1860 Mr. Lincoln received the committee that officially notified him of his candidacy for the presidency, and here on February 6, 1861, took place the last social event of Mr. Lincoln's life in Springfield.

Mr. Bowen gives the tenants of the house from February, 1861, when the Lincolns left it, until 1887 when it became State property, as follows: L. Tilton, George H. Harlow, Dr. Gustav Wendlandt, and O. H. Oldroyd. Mr. Tilton was president of the Great Western Railroad, the pioneer steam railroad of Illinois and now a part of the Wabash. He moved to Chicago shortly previous to the great fire of 1871 in which was destroyed much of the original Lincoln furniture.

George H. Harlow was a New Yorker and is chiefly known as one of the founders of the Union League of America. He and his family occupied the place until 1880, when Dr. Wendlandt, a physician and publisher of a German paper, moved in. The Wendlandts remained until 1883 when O. H. Oldroyd took charge. The Oldroyds occupied the house until 1893. While living here Mr. Oldroyd admitted visitors freely to the house, permitting them to view his great collection of Lincoln relics. In 1887 Robert T. Lincoln gave the house to the State, Mr. Oldroyd remaining as curator. In 1893 Governor Altgeld directed Oldroyd to vacate the premises, which he did, taking with him his collection. He soon "received an offer to take the collection to Washington and place it in the house in which

Lincoln died." He accepted and thus the collection that should today be in Springfield is in the national capital.

In the years since Lincoln's death the threshold of this house has felt the tread of countless thousands who have come to this comparatively simple home to pay homage to the great soul who once breathed the air within its walls. With his own hands he planted that stalwart elm that stands near the parking. Many a time did he romp down those steps to the street, his rollicking boys hanging to his long arms or swung atop his broad shoulders. In summer he read the papers or books upon that side porch or lay sprawled out upon the floor to romp with his lads. Often, it is said, the boys endangered the collection of shells on the corner "what-not," just as Herndon says they ruined the pens, spilled ink, and mixed papers, unrestrained by their father, at the office. If Lincoln was a superman out in the world, pleading before the Supreme Court or addressing the crowds in political meetings, here he was a plain humble citizen, happy in the companionship of his family.

I think a visit to this home comes nearer giving one a glimpse of the great homely frame of the man and the plain honesty of him than any spot connected with his life. And this is just the place to which Lloyd George, Joffre, Viviani, Clemenceau, King Albert of the Belgians, and countless other great men and women have come to sense the spirit of him who was a friend to all men. But most important of all is that constant throng of common folk, the kind of people whom Lincoln loved and who loved Lincoln, that come day in and day out, year in and year out, to pay humble tribute to him at the place that knew him most intimately. This is one of the great shrines of earth!

Hours: 10:00 A.M. to 12:00 M; 2:00 to 5:00 P.M. The house is closed on Sundays.

In 1843 Mr. Lincoln severed his association with

Judge Logan and formed the partnership with William Herndon which was to continue until his death. This change of firm again settled him on the west side of the square, in a building only a few feet away from the spot where he roomed with Speed when he first arrived in Springfield. Like the Speed store the site of this office is now occupied by Meyer Brothers store, in the show window of which establishment a tablet bearing this inscription will be seen:

1843 – 1861
LINCOLN & HERNDON
On this site stood a two-story
building. In a back room of
the second floor was the law office of
ABRAHAM LINCOLN
AND
WILLIAM H. HERNDON

Herndon describes the last meeting he had here with Lincoln just before the latter left Springfield for Washington. "He ran over the books," says Herndon, "and arranged for the completion of all unsettled and unfinished matters. . . . I never saw him in a more cheerful mood. He gathered a bundle of books and papers he wished to take with him and started to go; but before leaving he made the strange request that the signboard which swung on its rusty hinges at the foot of the stairway should remain. 'Let it hang there undisturbed,' he said, with a significant lowering of his voice. 'Give our clients to understand that the election of a President makes no change in the firm of Herndon and Lincoln. If I live I'm coming back some time, and then we'll go right on practising law as if nothing had ever happened.'"

Mr. Lincoln was not a member of any church but the family always maintained a pew in the First Presbyterian Church. Lincoln had been associated with this edifice from his early days in the city, speaking in the

building on many occasions. This old brick Greek
Revival church, with recessed porch and stalwart
Doric columns, stood at the southeast corner of Third
and Washington Streets. Business buildings now
occupy the site, but a tablet attached to the Washington
Street façade indicates Lincoln's association therewith
as follows:

1842 – 1861
SITE OF THE
FIRST PRESBYTERIAN CHURCH
IN WHICH
ABRAHAM LINCOLN
RENTED A PEW
1842 – 1861
AND WHERE THE FAMILY
ATTENDED SERVICE

There is a story current in Springfield to the effect
that on the Sunday after his nomination, Mr. Lincoln,
instead of strolling out with the boys, went to church
with Mrs. Lincoln. When Tad missed his father he
made a dash for the church and arrived, "disheveled,
ungartered and very grimy," about the middle of the
sermon. Mrs. Lincoln, elegantly attired, was visibly
embarrassed, but the President calmly stretched out a
long arm, gathering Tad into its shelter.

I do not know when the *old* First Presbyterian
Church was dismantled but it was still standing as late
as 1888. The present edifice stands but two squares
from the Lincoln Home on the northwest corner of
Seventh Street and Capitol Avenue. Near the front
of the auditorium is the old Lincoln pew from the
former church, appropriately decorated with American
flags at either end.

CHAPTER XII

The Eighth Judicial District
The Lincoln Circuit

WHILE Springfield was Lincoln's home from 1837 until he left for Washington, he was for months each year practising in the various county-seat towns of the old Eighth Judicial District. Starting soon after

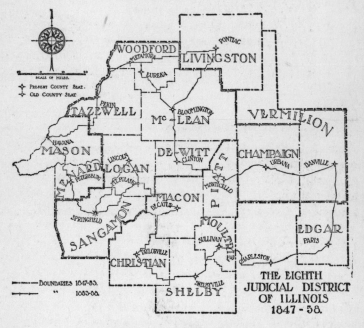

MAP OF THE LINCOLN CIRCUIT

his admission to the bar, he regularly made the rounds. At its greatest extent this district covered seventeen counties, but as it was constituted during the greater period of Lincoln's circuit-riding activity it included

142

STEPHENS COLLEGE,
COLUMBIA, MO.

A LINCOLN CIRCUIT COUNTY-LINE MARKER
Illinois

Photographs by the Author

LINCOLN-DOUGLAS PYRAMID
Near Monticello, Illinois

the following counties: Sangamon, Tazewell, Woodford, McLean, Logan, De Witt, Piatt, Champaign, Vermilion, Edgar, Shelby, Moultrie, Macon, and Christian. The district thus designated remained intact until 1853 when it was reduced to eight counties.

In this district, as in all others, court was held twice a year, in the spring and fall, and the terms were so arranged as to come in regular order, thus enabling the judge to move readily from one court to the next. With the judge went the bar, for few counties provided enough business to support the lawyers residing therein. It is said that Lincoln was the only lawyer who rode the entire circuit.

Court days were always great events in the Illinois towns of this period, and on these days everyone who could went to town. If the citizen was not on the jury, a witness or a suitor, he felt it his duty, nevertheless, to "go to court" to see and hear what was going on. When court was over in the evening, the judge, lawyers, and citizens congregated in the barrooms of the taverns where "yarns" were told and the evening spent in conversation of a nature regarded as highly entertaining by the old timers.

Judge David Davis, whom Mr. Lincoln later appointed as a Justice of the Supreme Court of the United States, and who presided in the Eighth District for a great part of the time during which Mr. Lincoln practised here, once said:

"I enjoyed for over twenty years the personal friendship of Mr. Lincoln. We were admitted to the bar about the same time and traveled for many years what is known in Illinois as the Eighth Judicial Circuit. In 1848 when I first went on the bench, the circuit embraced fourteen counties, and Mr. Lincoln went with the Court to every county. Railroads were not then in use and our mode of travel was either on horseback or in buggies."

Much discussion has arisen as to Lincoln's success

and popularity as a lawyer. "Contrary to a widely held belief," says Paul M. Angle, "Lincoln was not in great demand as a criminal lawyer, for in comparison with the rest of his business, his criminal work was almost negligible. Contrary to another popular belief, Lincoln was by no means the most popular lawyer on the circuit, at least in volume of business. . . . To the vexing question of Lincoln's capacity as a lawyer, existing court records provide no definite answer. They indicate, but do not prove, that in actual trial work Lincoln was no more successful than many of the lawyers who practised with him. However, in the higher court—the state supreme court and the United States courts at Springfield and Chicago—Lincoln had an enviable record. It is doubtful if any lawyer has ever surpassed his record in the supreme court."

Judge Davis once said that "in all the elements that constitute a great lawyer, he had few equals. . . . He seized the strong points of a cause and presented them with clearness and great compactness His mind was logical and direct and he did not indulge in extraneous discussion. . . . The frame-work of his mental and moral being was honesty, and a wrong cause was poorly defended by him. In order to bring into full activity his great powers it was necessary that he should be convinced of the right and justice of the matter which he advocated. When so convinced, whether the cause was great or small, he was usually successful. He hated wrong and oppression everywhere, and many a man whose fraudulent conduct was undergoing review in a court of justice has writhed under his terrific indignation and rebukes."

One of Mr. Lincoln's most important cases was that of the Illinois Central Railroad against the County of McLean (17 Ill., 291) which case involved the right of McLean County to tax lands of the Illinois Central Railroad in that county. It seems that Mr. Lincoln had been approached by some county officials regard-

Bloomington Sept 12. 1853.

T. R. Webber Esq—
My dear Sir:

On my arrival here to court, I find that McLean county has assessed the land and other property of the Central Railroad, for the purpose of county taxation. An effort is about to be made to get the question of the right to so tax the Co. before the court, & ultimately before the Supreme Court, and the Co. are offering to engage me for them— As this will be the same question I have had under consideration for you, I am somewhat trammelled by what has passed between you and me; feeling that you have the prior right to my services; if you choose to secure me at something near such as I can get from the other side— The question, in its magnitude, to the Co— on the one hand, and the counties in which the Co. has land, on the other, is the largest law question that can now be got up in the State; and therefore, in justice to myself, I can not afford, if I can help it, to miss a fee altogether— If you choose to release me, say so by return mail, and there an end— If you wish to retain me, you better get authority from your Court, come directly over in the Stage, and make common cause with this county—

Very truly your friend
A. Lincoln—

A PREVIOUSLY-UNPUBLISHED LINCOLN LETTER

ing his handling of the opposite side of this case for the
various counties interested.   The letter, shown herewith, indicates how fair Mr. Lincoln was.   He desired
to get a good fee; the railroad company would pay
such, but he felt that the counties had a prior right to
his services, if they could command them.   The letter
reads as follows:

Bloomington, Sept. 12, 1853.

T. R. Webber, Esq.
   My dear Sir:
   On my arrival here to court, I find that McLean county
has assessed the land and other property of the Central
Railroad, for the purpose of county taxation.   An effort is
about to be made to get the question of the right to so tax
the Co. before the court & ultimately before the Supreme
Court, and the Co. are offering to engage me for them.
As this will be the same question I have had under consideration for you, I am somewhat tramelled by what has
passed between you and me, feeling that you have the first
right to my services, if you choose to secure me a fee something near such as I can get from the other side.   The
question in its magnitude to the Co. on the one hand and
counties in which the Co. has land, on the other, is the
largest law question that can now be got up in the State;
and therefore, in justice to myself, I cannot afford, if I can
help it, to miss a fee altogether.   If you choose to release
me, say so by return mail, and then an end.   If you wish to
retain me, you better get authority from your Court, come
directly over in the Stage, and make common cause with
this county.
                    Very truly your friend,
                                    A. LINCOLN.

The foregoing letter was sent to Webber at Urbana.
He was clerk of Champaign County and a close friend
of Lincoln.   Mr. Lincoln was not retained by the
associated counties and he therefore took the case for
the Illinois Central.   The issue was a vital one for the
corporation since the claim of the counties would have
bankrupted the road at a time when it was still in the

detour from Route No. 8 at Washington (8 miles, "improved" road).

Another place prominent for its Lincoln associations is Bloomington, seat of McLean County. It was here that on May 29, 1856, the Republican party in Illinois was born. Mr. Lincoln's speech given in Major's Hall on that day is still regarded as one of the greatest ever delivered by him in Illinois and one that marked him out as a presidential possibility. So eloquent were his remarks and so spell-bound by his delivery were the reporters that they forgot to take notes and the result was that there is no record of his speech. For this reason it is referred to as Lincoln's "Lost Speech."

No one knows what Mr. Lincoln said on that occasion, although through the years several, like Henry C. Whitney, have set down what they thought they remembered. But that speech is lost and old Major's Hall, like the golden words of the speaker, has vanished.

Bloomington took an important place in the Lincoln-Douglas Debates of 1858, although no joint debate was held here. Mr. Douglas spoke at Bloomington July 16, and Mr. Lincoln was present to hear him. Lincoln spoke here on September 4, Douglas following with a second address on October 22.

On the occasion of Mr. Lincoln's speech he lodged with his friend Judge Davis and a procession of cheering backers marched to the home of the Judge to receive their hero. They then counter-marched to the Court House Square where, amid a great demonstration, Mr. Lincoln addressed about seven thousand hearers. On this appearance the speaker's remarks were recorded but no Bloomington man who had heard Lincoln two years before ever believed that he was half so eloquent upon this occasion.

It was in this same court house (since replaced) that Mr. Lincoln penned his brief but famous "Autobiography," written at the request of Jesse Fell in

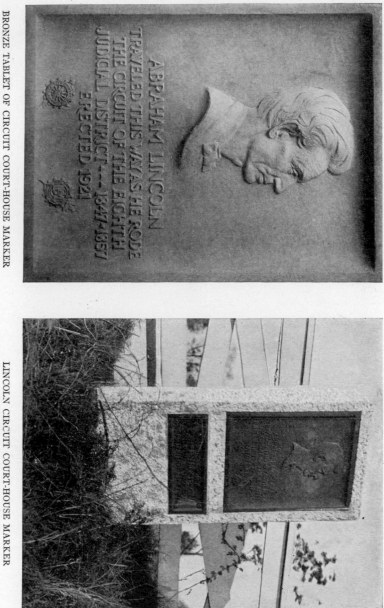

BRONZE TABLET OF CIRCUIT COURT-HOUSE MARKER
GEORG LOBER, SCULPTOR

LINCOLN CIRCUIT COURT-HOUSE MARKER
HENRY BACON, ARCHITECT

December, 1859, and here also his body lay in state on its memorable trip home after his assassination.

From Bloomington one may take Route No. 4 southwestward to Lincoln (32 miles) and on to Springfield (30 miles); Route 2 southward to Clinton (23 miles) and Decatur (26 miles) or Route 39 southeastward to Urbana (52 miles) and Danville (33 miles).

Lincoln, the present seat of Logan County, was not the original county capital, this being, upon the formation of the county in 1839, located at Pottsville. A court house, still standing, was built in 1840 and in this from 1840 to 1848 Mr. Lincoln practiced law as he rode the circuit. In 1848 the seat of government was removed to Mt. Pulaski, where the second court house was built. This town is reached from Lincoln over an "improved" road (11 miles). In 1852, when the Alton Railroad was built within a mile of Pottsville, a new town, named for the popular Springfield lawyer, was laid out by Mr. Lincoln's friends. The next year Lincoln, the first town named for the President before he attained national fame, was made the county seat. Thus Mr. Lincoln practiced law in three of the court houses of Logan County. Two of these, the early one in Pottsville (now a part of Lincoln) and that at Mt. Pulaski, still stand. Mr. Douglas spoke at Lincoln during the debates of '58 on September 4; Mr. Lincoln did not appear here.

Clinton, the seat of De Witt County and a regular point on the Lincoln Circuit, lies directly east of Lincoln. Both Lincoln and Douglas spoke here during the debates, Douglas opening his tour here on the afternoon of July 27, Mr. Lincoln attending the meeting and speaking that night at the court house. Lincoln spoke here again on September 2. On May 30, 1922, a Lincoln Circuit marker was erected in the courthouse yard.

Decatur has the honor of being the town in Illinois to which the Lincolns came on their arrival from

Indiana in 1830. That story has been told elsewhere. During his circuit-riding years Mr. Lincoln was often at Decatur where John Hanks, his kinsman and comrade of flatboat days, resided. When the days of Lincoln's political success came in 1860, Decatur took an important place. It was here that the Republican State Convention of 1860 met and here that the appelation of "Railsplitter" was forever attached to his name.

In the spring of 1860 Lincoln had delivered his famous Cooper Institute speech in New York City and had added to his string of successes a series of addresses in important New England cities. When he returned home the state convention was only five weeks off and the national convention six weeks away. Lincoln's friends were confident that he could be nominated for president in Illinois but they wanted to make such a demonstration that his name would be brought clearly before the eyes of the nation and *this* on the eve of the Chicago Convention. Mr. Lincoln attended the convention at Decatur on May 9 and 10.

Richard J. Oglesby, later governor of the state and a warm friend, conceived a slogan by which he thought Lincoln could be given great publicity, especially with the common people of the nation. He knew that Lincoln had split rails in this section thirty years before. So he hunted up John Hanks, who lived in the vicinity of the old Lincoln farm, ten miles west of Decatur, and together they secured two of the original rails that John said Lincoln had split in the winter of 1830–31. These were stored in Oglesby's barn, so the story goes, until convention day.

At the psychological moment Oglesby arose and announced that an old Democrat wished to make a contribution to the convention, and in came John Hanks, with helpers bearing aloft the two rails bearing the legend:

ABRAHAM LINCOLN
THE RAIL CANDIDATE
FOR PRESIDENT IN 1860.

Needless to say the convention went wild, and from
that moment on there was no question about the
popularity of Abraham Lincoln. The rails went down
as the campaign emblem and the name of "Old Abe
the Railsplitter" resounded throughout the nation!

Northeast of Decatur on Route 10 (32 miles) is
Monticello, an old Lincoln Circuit county-seat. Lincoln had warm friends here and many Lincoln stories
connect themselves with the place. Just south of the
town on Route 10, a large concrete pyramid marks
the meeting place of Lincoln and Douglas on this road
July 29, 1858. (See Chapter XII). Mr. Douglas had
spoken at Monticello on that day. Mr. Lincoln was
not to speak there until September 6.

From Monticello Route 10 leads north and east to
Champaign and Urbana, twin cities and the seat of
the University of Illinois. Urbana, the original town
and county-seat was founded in 1831. When the
Illinois Central built south through this section the
station (West Urbana) was established two miles west
of the town. This formed the nucleus for the modern
city of Champaign.

Lincoln was much at Urbana and had several legal
friends here, among them Henry C. Whitney and
Judge J. O. Cunningham, both of whom did much to
keep green the Lincoln memories. It was the latter
who made possible, through his will, the gift to Urbana
of Lorado Taft's noble bronze of Lincoln unveiled on
July 3, 1927. This splendid figure of Mr. Lincoln as
he must have looked during his circuit days in the
town stands in an attractive park facing the High
School, an everlasting inspiration to the youth of the
city. It seems quite appropriate that Urbana should
have this splendid work by Mr. Taft for his own first
impulse toward an artistic career came while he was a

student at the University in which his father was a professor and from which he graduated. The University owns a Lincoln memento of which it is proud. This is an ox-yoke made by the hand of "The Railsplitter." (In the University Library)

Urbana's present-day court house, the major portion of which dates from 1901, is in reality a remodeling of an old structure which in part dates back to Lincoln's time. This building, originally constructed in 1849 was, in 1859, amplified by the addition of two-story wings. Around this nucleus was erected the present-day structure. In the fall of 1854 Mr. Lincoln delivered an address upon the Nebraska Bill in the building. Judge Cunningham later had erected the white marble tablet at the right of the entrance to the County Clerk's suite on the second floor. It reads:

> On this spot Abraham Lincoln
> on October 24, 1854 delivered
> his third speech in opposition
> to Senator Douglas and the
> Nebraska Bill.

A few years ago Urbana erected a community hotel upon the site of the "old Kerr Tavern" at which, it is said, Lincoln lodged when in the town. The hostelry (Intersection of Routes 10 and 25) is appropriately called the "Urbana-Lincoln." Thomas Kerr, the aged son of the keeper of the tavern maintains, however, that it was "precious few times" that Lincoln lodged here, as the Kerrs, who came from the South, were all staunch Douglas men. It is definitely known that Mr. Lincoln also stayed at the old Urbana House, later known as the "Pennsylvania Hotel" which stood on the corner across the street east from the present county jail.

Mr. Lincoln spoke on numerous occasions in Urbana, one of his appearances still remembered by the old

THE LINCOLN STATUE AT URBANA, ILLINOIS
Unveiled June, 1927
LORADO TAFT, SCULPTOR

settlers being that of 1856 during the Fremont-
Buchanan campaign. In 1858 Mr. Douglas spoke
here on September 23, being followed by Mr. Lincoln
on the twenty-fourth. The "debaters" had just come
from Charleston, where on the Saturday previous
(September 18) they held their famous "fourth joint-
debate."

Today a modern concrete highway (Route 10)
leads from Urbana eastward to Danville (33 miles)
but the "old State Road" of that day is the rambling
thoroughfare that roughly parallels Route 10 at a
distance of about a mile south therefrom. About
nineteen miles east of Urbana this highway passes the
farm of John R. Thompson (1830–96), founder of the
line of metropolitan restaurants bearing his name.
Here a stone similar to the county-seat markers bears
the added legend:

IN MEMORY
JOHN R. THOMPSON
1830 – 1896
A FRIEND OF LINCOLN

Danville, the seat of "old Vermilion" was an important place in Lincoln's practice. Here resided
Ward Hill Lamon, his resident partner, who looked
after local interests. Lincoln, along with the "court,"
Judge Davis, Henry Whitney, and others, "would
come into town from Urbana, along in the afternoon,"
says Clint Clay Tilton,* "and put up at the old
McCormick Tavern, where a crowd was sure to be on
hand to welcome them." Lincoln would go into conference with Lamon at his office in the Barnum building (present site of the First National Bank) because
he had to get in hand the large number of cases usually
awaiting him. Judge Davis has recorded that often
Mr. Lincoln would appear on one side or the other of

* "Genesis of Old Vermilion," Jour. Ill. State Hist. Soc. April,
1927.

every case on the docket, and at Danville he pitted himself against some of the best minds of the Illinois and Indiana Bars.

Pekin, Paris, Charleston, Shelbyville, Taylorville, Petersburg, Havana, Hillsboro, and other old Illinois county-seat towns have their connections with Lincoln's legal life and a wealth of tradition and lore resulting therefrom. It would be futile to attempt to recount all of this but in nearly every one of these towns there are local-history students and newspaper men with a bent for history who ferret out such lore and retell it. And most of the towns, through the leadership of the Daughters of the American Revolution or some other patriotic agency, have marked the spots connected with this interesting phase of the Great Emancipator's life.

THE OLD COURT-HOUSE, PARIS, ILLINOIS

CHAPTER XIII

Scenes of the Lincoln-Douglas Debates

WHEN in 1854 Senator Douglas' Kansas-Nebraska Bill was passed by Congress, Abraham Lincoln was busy with the law on the Eighth Judicial Circuit. In his own words, "I was losing interest in politics when the repeal of the Missouri Compromise aroused me again." The Missouri Compromise, it was supposed, had settled for all time the question of the northern boundary of slavery in the West. With this question again open, Lincoln renewed his interest in politics, campaigning for Fremont in 1856 and entering the race for the senatorship against Douglas in 1858.

On June 17, 1858, the Republican State Convention nominated Lincoln as candidate for the senatorship and in response Mr. Lincoln delivered his famous "house divided against itself" speech. This speech defined Lincoln's stand and placed his doctrine in sharp contrast to that of Judge Douglas. On July 9, Douglas spoke at the Tremont House in Chicago and Mr. Lincoln was present to hear him. The next day Lincoln spoke in the same place but Senator Douglas did not attend. On the sixteenth Mr. Douglas spoke at Bloomington and Lincoln went thither to hear him. On July 17 both spoke at Springfield, Douglas in the afternoon, Lincoln in the evening. Neither heard the other. All this time, however, the country lawyer was making a detailed study of the methods and arguments of the wily politician.

The issue between them came to a definite head when, on July 24, Mr. Lincoln, then at the Tremont House in Chicago, sent to Mr. Douglas a formal chal-

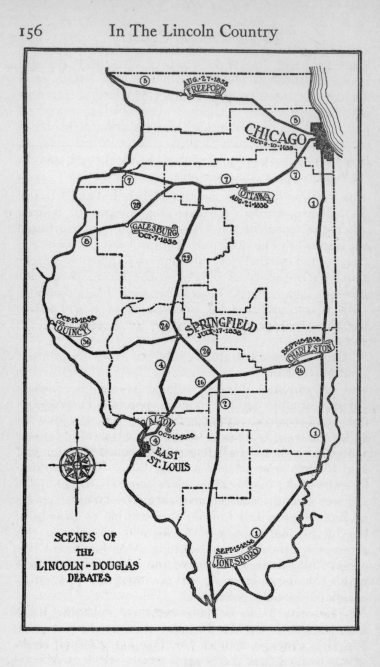

SCENES OF
THE
LINCOLN - DOUGLAS
DEBATES

lenge to cover the state together in a joint debate. Douglas' program for the campaign was pretty well arranged at the time and this fact he communicated to Mr. Lincoln. Nevertheless he felt able to accept in part Lincoln's challenge and made a counter proposal to which Mr. Lincoln agreed. After a meeting at Bement in Piatt County, Senator Douglas wrote Lincoln the final terms of the encounter as follows:

Dear Sir:—Your letter dated yesterday, accepting my proposition for a joint discussion at one prominent point in each Congressional District, as stated in my previous letter, was received this morning.

The times and places designated are as follows:—

Ottawa, La Salle County....	August	21st, 1858
Freeport, Stephenson County.	"	27th, "
Jonesboro, Union County....	September	15th, "
Charleston, Coles County....	"	18th, "
Galesburg, Knox County....	October	7th, "
Quincy, Adams County......	"	13th, "
Alton, Madison County......	"	15th, "

I agree to your suggestion that we shall alternately open and close the discussion. I will speak at Ottawa one hour, you can reply, occupying an hour and a half, and I will follow for half an hour. At Freeport, you shall open the discussion and speak one hour; I will follow for an hour and a half, and you can then reply for half an hour. We will alternate in like manner in each successive place.

Very respectfully, your obedient servant,

S. A. DOUGLAS.

Hon. A. Lincoln, Springfield, Illinois.

The old house at Bement from which Mr. Douglas wrote the above letter is still standing and is open as a Lincoln-Douglas memorial. This was the home of Mr. and Mrs. F. E. Bryant, cousins of William Cullen Bryant, the author, and pioneer settlers in Illinois. Mr. Bryant was a staunch friend of Douglas and when it was learned that the Senator was to speak at Monticello on July 29, the Bryants invited Mr. and Mrs. Douglas to be their guests while in Piatt County. Douglas had just opened his campaign for re-election at Clinton on the twenty-seventh, where Mr. Lincoln again attended his address and himself spoke in the evening.

The Douglases probably arrived at Bement on the Great Western Railroad the evening before. At any rate, on the morning of July 29 the Bryants and Douglases in the Bryant carriage drove to Monticello where the Senator was to speak in the afternoon. At that time Monticello had no railroad. At the conclusion of the meeting the party started back to Bement and, when about a mile south of Monticello, they met Mr. Lincoln on the road. "After passing the usual time of day," says Mr. J. F. Sprague, grandson of Mr. Bryant, "Senator Douglas said to Mr. Lincoln, 'Did you receive my letter?' Mr. Lincoln replied that he had. Senator Douglas then asked what he thought of it, to which Mr. Lincoln said he thought favorably of it, asking where he might confer with him after his return to Bement. Mr. Lincoln also had a political engagement in Monticello. Grandfather Bryant invited Mr. Lincoln to meet his guest, Senator Douglas, at his home in Bement." This spot on the road is today marked by the concrete pyramid mentioned in Chapter XII.

"When Lincoln returned to Bement he went to the place agreed upon, entering the little parlor . . . where Senator Douglas awaited him, going over in detail for some two hours" the arrangements for the joint debates. Mr. Lincoln took the midnight train west to Springfield. The next morning the Senator sent Lincoln the written confirmation of their agreement above quoted. The house was on July 29, 1925, donated to the community by Mr. Sprague as a memorial to the two giants who here agreed to hold this, one of the greatest forensic encounters in our

BRYANT HOUSE, BEMENT, ILLINOIS
Exterior
Photograph by the Author

BRYANT HOUSE, BEMENT, ILLINOIS
The Room in which Mr. Douglas and Mr. Lincoln formally agreed to meet in Joint Debate

history. The little parlor still retains its furniture of 1858.

It is not my intention to review the debates but simply to give the traveler seeking out the spots connected with Lincoln's life data regarding these places. Ottawa, the site of the first joint debate, we have noticed in Chapter VIII because of its earlier connection with Lincoln's life. On the morning of August 21, 1858, a special Rock Island train of some fourteen loaded coaches left Chicago for Ottawa. At Morris Mr. Lincoln boarded the train which reached Ottawa at 11:45. A delegation from Ottawa was at the same time proceeding along the Peru Road to meet Mr. Douglas who drove across the country in an open barouche drawn by four horses. The Senator was escorted to the Geiger House, attended by a large crowd.

Ottawa was at the time a town of about nine thousand souls. Its mayor was a Mr. Glover, a staunch Republican, who entertained Lincoln at his pleasant brick residence. The speaker's stand was erected in the public square—Lafayette Square—nicely wooded today but at that time almost devoid of shade. The weather was extremely hot, the dust was deep in the streets and no seats were provided for the audience. In spite of this, a great throng, arriving in buggies, on trains, horseback, and canal boats, swarmed around the stand at two o'clock. "Notwithstanding the heat," says Frank Stevens in his "Life of Douglas," "at least twelve thousand people had come to Ottawa to listen. They began pouring into the place before daylight. . . . Two brass bands paraded the streets. Militia companies followed. Flags, streamers, mottoes, and every manner of device which would float to the breeze, hung from windows and over the streets. Salutes were fired from two brass 12-pounders and the great red-letter day was enjoyed without manifestation of discomfort."

Freeport was the scene of the second debate; six days later and, this being far north in the state and in territory presumably not cordial to the Douglas doctrine, Lincoln took occasion to propound to the Senator a series of questions the answers to which are still known as the "Freeport heresy." Great importance has been attached to Douglas' answers, some even asserting that they "split the Democratic National Convention at Charleston in 1860 and made impossible the election of Douglas as president." Be that as it may, it was an important event for Freeport and the state, and, in spite of the fact that the weather had reversed itself, becoming suddenly cold and rainy, the crowd was even larger than at Ottawa. It is estimated that fully twenty thousand people from all over northern Illinois crowded into the town of about seven thousand population.

Senator Douglas arrived on Thursday evening from Galena, and Lincoln came from Mendota, arriving about ten o'clock on the morning of the debate. Both reception committees lodged their guests at the Brewster Hotel at the corner of Stephenson and Mechanic Streets, then a fine new hostelry recently opened. The speaker's stand was erected in a grove two squares in the rear of the hotel at a point then in the outskirts of the town. A marker was erected here in 1903 by the Freeport Woman's Club. President Roosevelt was present and on June 3 dedicated the monument, consisting of a large boulder to which a bronze tablet is attached.

Again in 1922 Freeport celebrated the sixty-fourth anniversary of the great event. With the help of automobiles and good roads the crowd was even larger than at the debate itself. Pageants, parades, oratory and fireworks served to revive memories of the old days. Freeport is on Illinois State Route No. 5 (Atlantic-Yellowstone-Pacific Highway) leading west from Chicago and is 28 miles west of Rockford.

The third debate was held at Jonesboro, the seat of Union County, "down in Egypt." This, on September 15, was the least attended of all the joint debates. Douglas had said that when he got Lincoln down to Egypt he would "bring him to his milk." "Jonesboro is the heart of Egypt," remarked the *Chicago Press and Tribune* of the 15th, "and here, if ever, the little giant will exhibit himself in the character of milkmaid. It is altogether probable that both himself and his milking arrangements will come out of the trial badly damaged."

Henry C. Whitney made the trip down with Lincoln. Here Lincoln acquitted himself well but was so worn by the trip and his debate that he decided to stay with a friend at Anna (1½ miles distant) for a day's rest before going north to Centralia, where he was to meet Jesse K. Dubois at the State Fair. He sent Whitney to Centralia and himself came up on the seventeenth, spending the day at the fair, as did Judge Douglas.

Whitney says that at Centralia Lincoln emerged from the train "alone with his carpet-bag and umbrella," while Douglas and his retinue were furnished with a private car by the officials of the Illinois Central Railroad. To his train was attached a platform car bearing Douglas' cannon which at every station "woke the echoes of enthusiasm for the destroyer of the time-honored Missouri Compromise."

On the evening of the seventeenth Lincoln and his friend went north to Mattoon en route to Charleston, where the fourth joint debate was scheduled for the eighteenth. Both Lincoln and Douglas lodged at Mattoon for the night, each being conducted to Charleston by his respective delegation in the morning. By Friday evening the hotels of Charleston were crowded and the streets were hung with flags and banners, and early on Saturday morning delegations from the adjoining precincts, and even from Indiana, began to arrive. By ten o'clock the streets were well-nigh impassable and the dust stifling. The chief decoration of the city was a gigantic banner eighty feet long, hung across the street from the Court House to a building opposite. On one side was inscribed:

COLES COUNTY
FOUR HUNDRED MAJORITY FOR LINCOLN.

On the reverse was a painting of "Old Abe Thirty Years Ago," driving three yoke of oxen hitched to a Kentucky wagon.

The Lincoln procession was about a mile long and had as a feature a wagon bearing thirty-two young ladies representing the states. The wagon bore this motto:

"Westward the Star of Empire takes its way,
The Girls Link-on to Lincoln—
As their Mothers linked to Clay."

Mr. Lincoln was lodged at the Capitol Hotel, while Judge Douglas was escorted to the Union House. The debate was held at the Fair Grounds where Lincoln sprung a coup by requiring O. B. Ficklin, "a right-hand man of Douglas," to bear witness to Lincoln's Congressional record, thereby making Douglas' attack on that record appear ridiculous. The effect upon the audience was marked and the speaker was given cheer after cheer. Thus ended one of the most rousing of the debates. Charleston is the seat of Coles County, 13 miles east of Mattoon and 28 miles west of Paris on Route 16.

The contest at Galesburg followed next, coming on October 7. This time the encounter was held under the classic influence of an academic setting, for the speaker's stand was erected against the east wall of the "Old Main Hall" of Knox College. In spite of stormy weather and a high wind which tore the banners and sent "signs pell-mell all over town," there were some twenty thousand people in attendance. Mr. Douglas arrived on the Burlington train from the west at 10:00 A.M. and was escorted to the Bancroft House and from there to the Bonny House, where a reception was held. Mr. Lincoln was escorted into town from Knoxville by a large delegation from that place and received at the residence of Henry R. Sanderson. Both speakers were presented with silken banners by their admirers.

Numberless banners made the town festive, those brought in by the Monmouth delegation being particularly clever because of their sketches and slogans. The south front of the college building at Knox carried a great banner lettered "KNOX COLLEGE GOES FOR LINCOLN," while directly over the speaker's stand at the east end was another: "KNOX COLLEGE FOR LINCOLN." The debate took place at two o'clock. That evening the Monmouth Glee Club sang amusing songs, some of which, written after the debate, "took off laughable episodes connected therewith."

Just fifty years after this famous debate, Knox College celebrated the event. A platform was erected upon the same spot and Chauncey M. Depew, ex-Governor Palmer, and Robert T. Lincoln were the speakers. Galesburg, a thriving city of twenty-five thousand is the home of Lombard College as well as of Knox College. The place was settled in 1836 by Rev. George Gale, an abolitionist. It is sixty miles north-west of Peoria and fifty-five miles east of Burlington, Iowa, on Route 8.

Having come to the western side of the state the remaining two battles were fought here, the next at Quincy and the last at Alton. Quincy was at the time an important city and one of the state's principal river ports, although its population did not exceed ten thousand souls. Judge Douglas arrived from Augusta the evening before the debate and was escorted from the station to his hotel, the Quincy House, with a torchlight procession. The old Quincy House stood

where Hotel Newcomb now stands. Mr. Lincoln
arrived at nine o'clock on the important morning and
was escorted by a procession to Judge Browning's
residence, from the classic portico of which he replied
to the welcome extended him.

The debate was held in Washington Square (now
Washington Park) at a point almost opposite the old
Court House. A boulder on the grass today marks
the spot. In that day the square was weedy and un-
kempt and was surrounded by a high fence with turn-
stiles at the gates. The streets though unpaved were
graveled, and the city boasted some metropolitan im-
provements like the gas lights, just installed. She was
also very proud of her militia companies the "Blues"
and the "Quincy Guards." The crowd here did not
equal that at Galesburg but on the whole it was a gala
day for Quincy.

Two days later the giants met for their last encounter at Alton, that early center of abolition with its
memories of Lovejoy. One cannot help contrasting
this contest with that other near contest when Lincoln
and Shields came close to a duelling combat near this
city. Alton too is on the river and again railroads and
steamboat lines ran reduced-fare excursions. The
crowd, however, amounted to only about six thousand.

Messrs. Douglas and Lincoln, both of whom came
down the river from Quincy, arrived before daylight,
Mr. Lincoln being received at the Franklin House, Mr.
Douglas at the Alton. Bands were on hand from several
other cities and Springfield Cadets paraded the streets.
A paper of the day says, "By the hour of twelve the
great American people had taken possession of the
city. It went up and down the streets—it hurrahed
for Lincoln and hurrahed for Douglas—it crowded the
auction rooms—it thronged the stores of our merchants
—it gathered on the street corners and discussed politics—it shook its fists and talked loudly—it mounted
boxes and cried the virtues of Pain Killer—it mustered

O. H. BROWNING HOME, QUINCY, ILLINOIS
Where Lincoln was Entertained during the Debate of October 13, 1858

to the eating saloons and it did not forget the drinking
saloons—it was here, there, and everywhere, asserting
its privileges and maintaining its rights." The stand
was erected against the eastern (Market Street) side of
the City Hall.

"The seven joint debates constituted only a small
part of the hard work done by the rival candidates,"
says Frank E. Stevens. "Up one side of the state and
down the other, they drove and rode, Douglas as a
rule, in a special train gorgeously decorated with bunt-
ing, under the direct eye of George B. McClellan
(later general), then of the Illinois Central Railroad
Company, while Lincoln was forced to take belated
trains, freight trains and many times to find himself
side-tracked to let the showy special of Douglas fly
past him." Thus they labored, each covering the
territory which he felt most needed his message. They
spoke at county fairs, in court houses, in churches,
wherever a gathering could be had or a call was made.
From July to October it was a merry battle and,
although Lincoln was not the victor in this election,
he had laid a secure foundation for his future
performance.

CHAPTER XIV
The Sites of Lincoln's Achievement

THE old Capitol and its part in Lincoln's life have been mentioned before but further reference is necessary because it was here that so many events connected with his final achievement took place. In fact so important in Lincoln history has the "house divided against itself" speech become that one speaker has rather poetically referred to the old building as the "House of the House Divided."* The occasion of this speech was the Republican State Convention of 1858 at which convention Mr. Lincoln was endorsed as "the first and only choice of the Republicans of Illinois for the United States Senate as a successor of Stephen A. Douglas." Dr. Barton says that Lincoln "knew that he would be nominated" and took great pains with the speech "which he was there to deliver." He delivered that speech in the Hall of Representatives, on the evening of June 16, opening with these words, now famous:

Mr. President and gentlemen of the Convention: If we could first know where we are, and whither we are tending, we could better judge what to do, and how to do it. We are now far into the fifth year since a policy was initiated with the avowed object and confident promise of putting an end to slavery agitation. Under the operation of that policy, that agitation not only has not ceased, but has constantly augmented. In my opinion, it will not cease until a crisis shall have been reached and passed. 'A house divided against itself cannot stand.' I believe this government cannot endure permanently half slave and half free. I do not expect the Union to be dissolved; I do not expect the house

* Trans. Ill. State Hist. Soc. 1924—p. 141.

to fall; but I do expect it will cease to be divided. It will become all one thing, or all the other. Either the opponents of slavery will arrest the further spread of it, and place it where the public mind shall rest in the belief that it is in the course of ultimate extinction, or its advocates will push it forward till it shall become alike lawful in all the states, old as well as new, North as well as South.

Many students consider this the greatest speech ever delivered by Mr. Lincoln. Certainly it was masterful in construction and delivery—an utterance noble enough to make the hall which reverberated to its sound easily one of the choicest of the Lincoln shrines. Fortunate is it that we may stand below its classic pillars and reconstruct the scene at which Mr. Lincoln delivered the words that, it was predicted, would make him president!

The Republican National Convention of 1860 was held in the city of Chicago. At Decatur, just the week before, Abraham Lincoln had been put forth as the presidential choice of the Republican Party of Illinois. The contest promised to be a spirited one but the fact that the national convention was to be held in his own state was not without its weight. The Convention convened in the "Wigwam" on Market Street between Lake and Randolph and not far from where the newly constructed Wacker Drive joins Market today. This great wooden structure, entirely without beauty, structural or otherwise, was described by Horace Greeley, who came out from New York to report the convention for his paper. He said, "The Republicans have built a great structure which they call the Wigwam. God help the Indians if they ever lived in as ugly a building as this!" There used to be a tablet marking the site of the Wigwam, but I have not seen it for several years.

Most readers are familiar with the history that was made during this convention, with the great crowds the event attracted, and with the convention's outcome. There is no need to recount these. The convention assembled at noon on Wednesday, May 16, Mr. Seward's birthday. It seemed that Seward would without question be the general choice for nominee. Mr. Lincoln was not in attendance, but remained at home in Springfield, keeping, however, in close touch with the situation by telegraph.

Two days were consumed with the framing of a "platform" and on Friday morning a great fanfare of brass trumpets announced the procession of the Seward forces through the streets of Chicago to apparent victory at the Wigwam. The Lincoln supporters, however, had proceeded early to the building and when the Seward delegation arrived the Lincoln men were strongly entrenched in the seats. By ten o'clock the Wigwam was jammed to the doors and the crowd is said to have extended for some blocks down Market Street. Without a nominating speech William H. Evarts arose and nominated William H. Seward "for the office of President of the United States" and almost immediately Norman D. Judd arose and said:

"I desire on behalf of the delegation from Illinois to put in nomination as a candidate for President of the United States, Abraham Lincoln of Illinois."

The names of other candidates were put and balloting began almost immediately. Upon the third ballot, Mr. Lincoln secured all but 1½ votes necessary for nomination, but before the result could be finally checked, Carter of Ohio arose to announce a change of five votes from Chase to Lincoln. Changes now followed rapidly and at 12:30 P.M. the convention declared Mr. Lincoln nominated.

Aside from the Wigwam, perhaps the Tremont House which stood at the southeast corner of Dearborn and Lake Streets, recently the site of the Northwestern University Law School, was more intimately connected with Mr. Lincoln's success than other spots in the city. Here he attended a party conference

(April, 1854) and the Republican banquet of December 10, 1856; here on July 10, 1858, he made his speech replying to that of Douglas of the night before, and here on the following 24th he wrote the challenge which resulted in the Lincoln-Douglas Debates. The spot is today marked by two tablets, one quoting a portion of his remarks made at the Alton Debate. It is presumable that while in Chicago on business Mr. Lincoln often stayed at the Tremont, although we know that he sometimes put up at the old Sherman House. His last appearance was on Friday, November 23, 1860, when a reception was held in the parlors of the hotel for Mr. and Mrs. Lincoln and Hon. Hannibal Hamlin in order that Chicagoans might "see the gallant standard-bearers of Republicanism."

While the convention was in session at Chicago, Springfield was equally active in expectancy and, when the news of Lincoln's nomination was flashed over the wires of the old Illinois and Mississippi Telegraph Company, the town went wild. Clinton Conkling has told this story of how Mr. Lincoln first received the good news. Lincoln had just finished a long conference with James C. Conkling who had returned from two days at Chicago. "In a very few moments after Mr. Lincoln left," says Conkling, "I learned of his nomination . . . and rushed after him. I met him on the west side of the square before anyone else had told him, and to my cry, 'Mr. Lincoln, you're nominated!' he said, 'Well, Clinton, then we've got it,' and he took my outstretched hand in both of his. Then the excited crowds surged around him and I dropped out of sight."

This is only one of several versions of the story as told in Springfield. I have no notion of what are the facts in the matter and I do not know that it makes much difference. We do know, however, that on the following Saturday a special train from Chicago bore to Springfield the delegation appointed formally to notify Mr. Lincoln. This delegation he received at his home (See Chapter XI).

Mr. Lincoln did not take a speaking part in the campaign of 1860 but remained quietly in Springfield attending to the many details that a campaign entails and meeting the individuals and delegations who came to consult him. The little Lincoln-Herndon office could not accommodate this activity, and Governor Wood graciously tendered the candidate the use of the executive offices on the second floor of the State House. Newton Bateman, then Superintendent of Public Instruction, occupied the office next to the Governor's suite and on many occasions the overflow from Mr. Lincoln's rooms had to be accommodated in his office. Dr. Bateman, afterward president of Knox College, had many stories about this period of Mr. Lincoln's career, one involving the correction of Lincoln's formal reply to his nomination notification in which the presidential candidate had incorporated the split infinitive "to not violate." Dr. Bateman suggested the transposition of the "to" and the "not" to which Lincoln replied, "Oh, you think I had better turn those two little fellows end for end."

The summer wore on and the fall elections proved the wisdom of the Chicago Convention's choice. Mr. Lincoln was elected! Then came the formation of his cabinet and preparations for the removal to Washington in the spring. Late in January Mr. Lincoln began the writing of his inaugural address. "He asked me," said Herndon, "to furnish him with Henry Clay's great speech delivered in 1850; Andrew Jackson's proclamation against Nullification; and a copy of the Constitution. He afterwards called for Webster's reply to Hayne . . . which he always regarded as the grandest specimen of American oratory. With these few 'volumes,' and no further sources, he locked himself up in a room upstairs over a store across from the State House, and there, cut off from all communication and intrusion, he prepared the address. Though composed amid the unromantic surroundings of a dingy, dusty, and neglected back room, the speech has become a memorable document."

That "dingy dusty backroom" of Lincoln's inspiration still remains and Lincoln students will want to visit the spot. It is located on the third floor rear of the building now occupied by B. H. Luers and Sons (528 East Adams Street). A tablet near the entrance by which one ascends the echoing stairway reads:

> Abraham Lincoln prepared and
> wrote his First Inaugural Address
> as President of the United States in
> the third story of this building in
> the month of January, 1861.

On the sixth of the following month the Lincolns attended the last social event of the President's life in Springfield. This was a reception in their own home tendered by Mr. and Mrs. Lincoln to their friends and neighbors. The *Missouri Democrat* reported the event as follows:

The first levee given by the President-elect took place last evening at his own residence . . . and it was a grand outpouring of citizens and strangers, together with the members of the legislature. . . . Mr. Lincoln threw open his house for a general reception of all the people who felt disposed to give him and his lady a parting call. The levee lasted from seven to twelve o'clock in the evening and the house was thronged by thousands up to the latest hour. Mr. Lincoln received the guests as they entered and were made known. They then passed on and were introduced to Mrs. Lincoln, who stood near the center of the parlor, and who . . . acquitted herself most gracefully and admirably. . . . She is a lady of fine figure and accomplished address and is well calculated to grace and to do honors at the White House.

Arranging for the renting of his property and the sale of his household effects, Mr. Lincoln is said to have taken his family to the old Chenery House, then a leading hotel of the city, where they lodged for a few days prior to leaving for the national capital. On the morning of his departure, so the story goes, he called at the Hotel office and procured several of the hotel cards upon which he wrote,

A. Lincoln,
White House,
Washington, D. C.

Tacking these upon his several trunks and declining the help of attendants, he roped the baggage and dispatched it to the railway station.

The morning (February 11, 1861) was rainy and disagreeable, but in spite of this a large gathering of friends, neighbors and townspeople were at the Great Western Passenger Station to bid the family farewell. Mr. Lincoln had not intended to make any parting remarks, but when he saw his old friends gathered about the car he stepped to the platform and bade them good-bye in the following beautiful words:

My friends: No one not in my situation can appreciate my feeling of sadness at this parting. To this place and the kindness of this people, I owe everything. Here I have lived a quarter of a century, and have passed from a young to an old man. Here my children have been born, and one is buried. I now leave, not knowing when or whether ever I may return, with a task before me greater than that which rested upon Washington. Without the assistance of that Divine Being who ever attended him, I cannot succeed. With that assistance, I cannot fail. Trusting in Him who can go with me, and remain with you and be everywhere for good, let us confidently hope that all will yet be well. To His care commending you, as I hope in your prayers you will commend me, I bid you an affectionate farewell.

The old Great Western Station, now the freight depot of the Wabash Railroad, stands on the corner of Tenth and Monroe Streets. This brick building

LINCOLN STATUE IN FRONT OF THE STATE CAPITOL
Springfield, Illinois
Andrew O'Connor, Sculptor

OLD GREAT WESTERN PASSENGER STATION, NOW WABASH FREIGHT HOUSE
Springfield, Illinois
Here Lincoln bade good-bye to Springfield after his election to the Presidency

Photographs by the Author

has now been raised to a two-story structure but otherwise it is little altered. A granite marker surrounded by an iron fence stands at the Monroe Street end of the depot. On the west side of the monument a bronze tablet records Mr. Lincoln's farewell remarks; on the east a tablet bears this inscription:

> The Site of the Great Western R. R. Passenger Station and near their track where stood the train from which President-elect Mr. Lincoln made his farewell address.

In the gray mist of that rainy winter morning the train threaded its way eastward, bearing Mr. Lincoln toward his high destiny.

CHAPTER XV

WASHINGTON—DEATH—THE JOURNEY HOME

THE story of those long years of national strife, the turmoil of civil war, the petty bickerings of small-minded politicians and the part Mr. Lincoln was called upon to take in it all is one too well known even to require casual reference. The country, war-worn and weary, looked forward to a day when the terrible strife would be passed. The black man had been set free and the wisdom of the President's leadership, so often disputed during the darkest days of the strife, were apparently endorsed by his re-election by a splendid majority in 1864.

Mr. Lincoln confidently looked forward to the solution of the war and prayed for its cessation, but he was perfectly conversant with the great problem of pacification and reconstruction that lay beyond the success of arms. He had been at the battle-front; he had investigated with deep interest the crying problems that he was called upon to solve. With that splendid affection and calm firmness always characteristic of him he set his hand to the task. In his second inaugural address, in my estimation one of his noblest utterances, he gave verbal form to the motives that then actuated him.

With malice towards none, with charity for all, with firmness in the right as God gives us to see the right, let us finish the work we are in, to bind up the nation's wounds, to care for him who shall have borne the battle and for his widows and orphans, to do all which may achieve and cherish a just and lasting peace.

The above words were uttered on March 4, 1865.

Then came the end of the war and the first fulfilment
of that for which he had prayed. Lee surrendered on
April 9 and five days later the President was shot
down by an assassin's bullet as he sat in a box at Ford's
Theatre.

Many stories come down to us through eye-wit-
nesses of this tragic event but there is little point in
repeating them. The President, as is well known, was
removed to the Peterson House directly across Tenth
Street, where at 7:22 on the morning of April 15 he
died. Secretary Stanton, often unappreciative of
his chief in life, is said to have remarked as he viewed
his body, quiet with death, "Now he belongs to the
ages!" and he later declared that Lincoln "was the
most perfect ruler of men the world has ever seen."

The house in which the President died still stands
today (516 Tenth Street). This old residence, later
thoroughly renovated, contains the famous Oldroyd
Memorial Collection of Lincolniana, once housed in the
Lincoln Home at Springfield. This collection, containing more than three thousand articles pertaining
to the martyred President, has among other things the
family Bible, a rail split by Lincoln in 1830, the office
chair he used while writing his first inaugural address
and some of the furniture of the Springfield house.

Visitors, perhaps, will wonder why the collection
was ever allowed to leave Springfield. I shall leave
Mr. Oldroyd to tell that story:*

I asked Mr. Conkling (Clinton Conkling) to request
Robert Lincoln to present the House to the State, and if he
did, I would present the collection at my death. Mr.
Conkling wrote to Robert and his reply was that he did not
like to offer it for fear it would appear as if he wanted to do it
for political purpose. I took the letter to Representative
Bogardus of Paxton and asked him to have a committee
appointed to negotiate with Robert. Mr. Lincoln then
offered it as a gift. The committee asked me that I would

* From a letter to L. A. Bowen of Springfield, dated Feb. 9, 1925.

keep the collection and take care of the house. I told them that, if the State paid me a reasonable salary, at my death the collection would go to the State as a gift. Two contracts were signed and the State has one and I the other.

Governor Altgeld* sent a messenger with an order for me to vacate the house within two weeks. I rented Dr. Ryan's house and stored the collection in it. I soon received an offer from a memorial committee in Washington which was created by congress for the purpose of preserving historic houses, to take the collection to Washington and place it in the house in which Lincoln died. I accepted the offer; for while I was sad at taking it away from Springfield there was not an effort upon the part of anyone in Springfield to have it remain. . . . I commenced the collection in 1860 during the presidential campaign and have been collecting ever since.

Illinois has since realized her loss in permitting this collection to leave the state and a recent Assembly appropriated $50,000 for its purchase. The federal government, however, through the efforts of H. M. Rathbone†, late congressman-at-large from Illinois, made a similar appropriation and Mr. Oldroyd accepted its offer. Thus, although this splendid collection is not to return to Illinois, it is to be properly safeguarded for all time. In addition to the Oldroyd Collection and that of the State Historical Library at Springfield, one of the most important in the country, the McClellan Collection at Brown University, the Gunther Collection of Chicago and the Judd Stewart (now the Henry Huntington) Collection of Pasadena, California, are notable.

Lincoln admirers visiting Washington must by all means see the Oldroyd Collection. The house is reached by F Street cars of the Washington Railway & Electric Co. or the Avenue cars of the Capitol Traction Co. (light green cars) and busses of the Rapid Transit Co. marked "8th & Penn Ave."

Ever since the Government purchased the old Ford

* This was three years later, early in 1893.
† Mr. Rathbone died July 16, 1928.

CARRIAGE USED BY PRESIDENT LINCOLN ON THE NIGHT OF HIS ASSASSINATION
In Museum of The Studebaker Corporation of America, South Bend, Indiana

Theatre it has served as office space for overcrowded governmental departments. Shortly before his recent death, Congressman Rathbone, whose grandfather was the Major Rathbone in the box with the President upon the night of his assassination, sponsored a bill asking Congress to appropriate funds to preserve the structure and provide housing for the Oldroyd Collection. The War Department and the Records and Patents Bureau, both of which have been using the structure, have no funds for its repair. It should by all means be preserved.

Joseph Christian, the coachman who drove the President's party to Ford's Theatre upon that fatal Good Friday of 1865, died recently. The old carriage which he drove upon that occasion is preserved in the collection of historic vehicles owned by the Studebaker Corporation of South Bend, Indiana, through whose courtesy the photograph herewith shown was procured.

Perhaps the grief of no people ever equaled that occasioned by the death of Mr. Lincoln. The rejoicing that followed the assurance of peace turned overnight to cries of lamentation. "It was," says Stoddard, "as if there had been a death in every house throughout the land. By both North and South alike the awful news was received with a shudder and a momentary spasm of unbelief. Then followed one of the most remarkable spectacles in the history of the human race, for there is nothing else at all like it on record. Bells had tolled before at the death of a loved ruler, but never did bells toll so mournfully as they did that day. Business ceased. Men came together in public meetings as if by a common impulse, and party lines and sectional hatreds seemed to be obliterated . . . on the following Sunday funeral services were held in all the churches in the land and every church was draped in mourning."

Appropriate funeral services were held at the White House, and on April 20 the body was placed under the

Rotunda of the Capitol where thousands tramped by
to look upon the tranquil brow of him who was a
friend of all the people. The next day the funeral
train left Washington for that memorably sorrowful
journey back to Lincoln's old home town. Everywhere
sorrowing thousands lined the tracks and in the great
cities other thousands tramped past his casket, eager
to pay him final respect. The train moved from
the Capital City to Baltimore, then to Harrisburg,
Philadelphia, New York, Albany, Buffalo, Cleveland,
Columbus, Indianapolis, Chicago, Bloomington, and
at last to Springfield. Upon the trip from Chicago to
Springfield Mr. Pullman put at the service of the
President's family and party the "Pioneer," the first
real "palace" car, which thus made its "maiden" trip
to Springfield in this connection. This seems significant
in view of the fact that Robert Lincoln later became
president of the Pullman Company.

A LITTLE-KNOWN PORTRAIT OF LINCOLN
BY GEORGE H. STORY
Property of Illinois State Historical Society

CHAPTER XVI

WHERE SPRINGFIELD RECEIVED HIM BACK

MEANWHILE the grief of his old friends and neighbors at Springfield knew no bounds. A few hours after the news of his death reached the city a great public meeting spontaneously assembled in the open air at the south front of the State House. Hon. Shelby M. Cullom called the meeting to order and suggested that Hon. J. K. Dubois act as chairman. He was chosen, and a body of vice-chairmen were elected to make the necessary funeral arrangements. Many important citizens, among them John T. Stuart and Stephen A. Logan, Mr. Lincoln's former legal partners, acted upon this committee.

The remains of the dead President reached Springfield on the third of May, accompanied by the members of the Cabinet, members of the United States Senate and House of Representatives; distinguished military officials and many important private citizens from other states. The train arrived over the Chicago and Alton Railroad and at the passenger station of that line at the corner of Third and Washington Streets. The station has since been replaced but an appropriate tablet marks the spot.

The remains, resting upon an appropriate and beautiful catafalque were taken to the old House of Representatives at the Capitol where upon so many occasions the honored dead had distinguished himself. Here, within the two days during which the body lay in state, over a hundred thousand sorrowing citizens of Illinois and neighboring states passed his bier.

"The Capital of Illinois," said Edward L. Merritt, editor of the *State Register*, and one of the secretaries

of the Springfield committee, "had made elaborate
preparations for the last offices of the dead. To con-
summate a becoming tribute of an affectionate people,
money, skill, patience, labor, nothing was spared that
Springfield's love offering should be worthy of her
great dead. The funeral obsequies of the mortal remains of Mr. Lincoln occurred on the 4th day of May,
1865, and no American ever, up to this time, was laid
to rest with more genuine love and distinguished and
beautiful honors. . . .

"The funeral pageant was the largest and most
imposing ever witnessed in the United States. It was
made up of military, professional, and about every
known fraternal and civic organization, embracing
eight divisions. All were afoot except the marshals,
their aids, and distinguished guests. The column of
marchers reached from curb to curb and in close order.
General Joseph E. Hooker was marshal in chief with
General John Cook . . . as chief of staff. The late
General John A. McClernand . . . was grand marshal, and rode at the head of the second division
followed by the hearse. . . . The cortège was of such
great numbers and of so great length that the head of
the procession had reached Oak Ridge where the remains of Mr. Lincoln were temporarily deposited in
the receiving vault of the cemetery, before more than
one-half of it was in line. In this march to the "City
of the Dead," scores upon scores of the best musical
organizations of the nation were in line, whose funeral
dirges cadenced the great wail of a bereft people."
Thus did the nation lay to rest her first martyred
President!

THE LINCOLN MONUMENT, SPRINGFIELD, ILLINOIS
The Burial-place of the Lincolns

Photograph by the Author

CHAPTER XVII
WHERE HE SLEEPS

ON THE day of the funeral the Lincoln National Monument Association was organized with the Hon. Richard J. Oglesby, Governor of Illinois, as president. Upon this day the first local contributions that were to make possible the final resting-place of the President were received. A contract was soon made for the purchase of ground where the present capitol stands, and the construction of a temporary receiving-vault was commenced. Mrs. Lincoln, however, was not favorable to that site, and at her suggestion Oak Ridge, a new cemetery at that time, was selected as a site for the monument. Here a temporary vault was constructed and the body of the President removed thereto on December 21, 1865.

The permanent monument was constructed under the direction of the Springfield Committee and the design selected for its construction was that of Larkin G. Mead (1835–1910), an American sculptor who spent a great deal of his life in Florence, Italy. Popular subscription supplied the major portion of the funds for its erection, donations coming from thousands of individuals and organizations throughout the country, nearly seventeen hundred Sunday schools making gifts. The State of Illinois appropriated $50,000, Missouri, $1,000, and Nevada $500. A touching tribute was the contribution of about $8,000 from the colored soldiers of the United States Army.

By the fall of 1871 the crypt of the permanent monument was completed and on September 17 the body was placed there. Construction continued and on October 9, 1874, the remains were placed in the sarcophagus at the center of the catacomb. The monument is constructed of brick faced with Quincy granite and consists of a podium 72 x 72 feet and 16 feet high. This encloses the catacomb at the north and a "memorial hall" at the south. Above this base the obelisk, eleven feet square, arises to a height of 135 feet above the sidewalk. The monument was originally 115 feet high but in 1901 it was increased to its present height.

The monument was dedicated October 15, 1874, at which time Governor Oglesby delivered an oration commemorative of the life and services of the Great Emancipator. President Grant was present and spoke briefly and James Judson Lord read a poem. Mead's statue of Mr. Lincoln, in bronze, stands at the base of the obelisk facing south, while the corners are flanked by groups in bronze representing the Infantry, the Navy, the Artillery, and the Cavalry, the first two groups being contributed by citizens of Chicago and New York City respectively.

In the late nineties it became apparent that the footings were not adequate as the foundations began to show signs of unequal settlement. This necessitated the restoration of the structure which was begun by Col. J. S. Culver in November, 1899. It was rebuilt from the foundation up, the footings being deepened by twenty-four feet.

On November 7, 1876, thieves attempted to steal the body of the President and shortly thereafter John Carroll Powell, custodian from 1874 until 1895, organized the "Lincoln Guard of Honor." The object of this guard was to safeguard the "precious dust of Abraham Lincoln from vandal hands and to conduct, upon anniversaries of his birth and death, suitable memorial exercises." At the time of restoration, a concrete vault was placed beneath the floor of the catacomb, directly under the sarcophagus, and in this vault the body of Mr. Lincoln was placed September 26, 1901. In the monument rest also the re-

LINCOLN STATUE, INNER DRIVE, GRANT PARK, CHICAGO, ILLINOIS, GENERAL VIEW
AUGUSTUS SAINT-GAUDENS, SCULPTOR

mains of Mrs. Lincoln, the sons and one grandson, a child of Robert T. Lincoln.

From October 15, 1874, until July 9, 1895, the monument remained in the control of the Monument Association. During all this time an admission fee of twenty-five cents was charged. In 1894 there arose a protest against this and the General Assembly made provision for the transfer of the property to the State. This transfer was made on July 9, 1895, by Richard J. Oglesby, first president of the Association and the only surviving member of the original body. The fee was abolished and the monument is open to the public from 8:00 A.M. to 6:00 P.M., Sundays included. Herbert Wells Fay, the custodian, has on display in the Memorial Hall, a Lincoln collection of over 26,000 items.

To reach the tomb visitors take North Fifth Street cars to Oak Ridge Cemetery or, by automobile, go north on Sixth Street following the signs that direct one to the "Lincoln Tomb." The increasing throng that each year comes to this shrine is testimony to the growing regard in which the greatest American is held.

OTHER LINCOLN MEMORIALS
AND SHRINES

CHAPTER XVIII

OTHER LINCOLN MEMORIALS AND SHRINES

PERHAPS no American, save Washington, has figured more widely in story and picture than Abraham Lincoln. He was photographed perhaps more often than any man of his day, and for this reason a great wealth of documentary material regarding his physical form comes down to us. Moreover, while still alive impressions were made of his face and hands, thus preserving for all time accurate data regarding these important features of the man. It has always seemed a strange coincidence that Leonard W. Volk, a relative by marriage of Douglas, should have been the medium through whom these documents have been preserved.

In 1857 Mr. Douglas sent Volk to Italy to complete his training as a sculptor and after he returned he essayed a bust of Mr. Lincoln. To this end he made a life-mask of Lincoln in Chicago in the spring of 1860. The hands he recorded at Springfield on Sunday, May 21, just after Mr. Lincoln's nomination. These "documents," it goes without saying, must form the basis of the studies of all artists who would, with anything like realistic effect, perpetuate the physical aspect of Lincoln.

At many places in this broad country stand monuments to and likenesses of this great American figure. While not to be compared with those shrines which are made sacred through intimate association with his life, these memorials are valuable in that they keep constantly before our people the staunch honesty and sterling nobility of the man. One of the noblest monuments to Lincoln yet erected is the Lincoln Memorial at Washington, of which Henry Bacon, a native of Illinois and once a student at the University of Illinois, was architect. This building is without doubt the greatest work of Mr. Bacon, who was as refined a classicist as America has produced. The splendid, serene figure in bronze that sits majestically upon its pedestal at the heart of this shrine is likewise one of the great figures of the martyred President and the work of Daniel Chester French. In a recent interview Thomas Clapham, the custodian, said: "There is something in the air here in the memorial, a feeling of greatness that I can't explain. . . . I believe it makes a man better to have seen it. I think it is one of the greatest institutions for good that we have." Yes, this is the purpose of all great memorials and it is the true mission of art to further these noble ends. The Lincoln Memorial is a splendid shrine, nobly conceived and brilliantly executed!

In this temple
As in the hearts of the people
For whom he saved the Union
The memory of Abraham Lincoln
Is enshrined forever.

Chicago has two splendid statues of Mr. Lincoln, one that majestic figure in Lincoln Park, the other a seated figure recently put in place after a period of twenty-five years storage in the Art Institute. Both are the works of the immortal Saint-Gaudens and both are great works of art. But for my part I like better the standing figure in Lincoln Park. I know it has been criticized for its lack of realism. But this statue of Lincoln was meant to be more than a photographic study of the man. It is the enshrining of a great soul, interpreted through the medium of another great soul. It is in short, Saint-Gaudens' Lincoln; not the plainsman Lincoln, not the lawyer, not the politician, but the majestic soul of Lincoln the Emancipator.

LINCOLN STATUE, INNER DRIVE, GRANT PARK, CHICAGO
AUGUSTUS SAINT-GAUDENS, SCULPTOR

I am not sure that it is materially, anatomically the Lincoln of reality any more than the Lincoln of Sandburg's writing is the Lincoln of *scientific* history. But it is Saint-Gaudens' conception of what the great Lincoln must have been in those supreme moments of his life when he arose to the great situations of that life. Someone has said of the Venus de Milo that "she is not what any Greek woman ever was; she is what every Greek woman would like to have been." That is, she is the Greek woman idealized. This then, was Saint-Gaudens' ideal Lincoln, a wonderful figure that gives to everyone who views it a nobler, a higher conception of the really great qualities in human nature.

Some have complained that this work should have gone to Volk because of his intimate relations with Mr. Lincoln, but in my estimation the works of Saint-Gaudens are finer in every respect than that of Volk at Rochester. The seated Lincoln has within two years been placed in an excellent setting near the Inner Drive in Grant Park and almost opposite the splendid new Buckingham Fountain.

On the campus of the University of Wisconsin a good likeness of Mr. Lincoln by Adolph Weinman, favorite pupil of Saint-Gaudens and the author of the figure in the rotunda of the State House at Frankfort, Kentucky, acquaints the students of that great university with the physical aspects of the man. Mr. Weinman was also the author of the Lincoln in the public square at Hodgenville not far from the birthplace of the President.

In a pretty little square known as Lytle Park in Cincinnati stands George Gray Barnard's gaunt and rugged figure of Lincoln, the raw-boned westerner. This conception, a gift to the city by Mr. Charles P. Taft, created considerable criticism at the time it was unveiled. It is the case in which the stark realities are emphasized to an extent out of proportion to their importance. Lincoln in repose, I have been told by people who knew him, did not impress people with his greatness. It was only when he was in action pleading a case, answering a Douglas, settling great problems, that his true nobility shone forth. But since it is *this inner greatness* which we seek—*this soul of the man*—it seems to me that a conception that does not convey a measure of this is scarcely worthy of its subject. Louisville has a replica of Barnard's figure. It stands near the Public Library. And London was to have had a copy but preferred a replica of Saint-Gaudens' Lincoln of Lincoln Park. The Barnard figure for London went to Manchester.

Many people have liked Charles J. Mulligan's Lincoln the Railsplitter (1911) in Garfield Park, Chicago, while others are equally fond of Gutzon Borglum's unconventional figure at Newark, New Jersey. It shows the President seated upon a classic bench, his tall hat beside him.

Most of the important sculptors of the last half century have essayed a Lincoln, and many of our cities have good likenesses of him. In this connection one should mention Andrew O'Connor's Lincoln in front of the Capitol at Springfield, the figure by Charles H. Neihaus at Buffalo, with a replica at Muskegon, Michigan; the essays of Henry K. Brown at Union Square, New York and in Brooklyn, the figure by Daniel Chester French at Lincoln, Nebraska, and that by Lorado Taft at Urbana, Illinois. There are other figures at Boston, Berkeley (California), Hartford, Takoma (Washington), Gettysburg, Columbus (Ohio), Omaha, and Edinburgh, Scotland, with still others under way at Cleveland, Jersey City, and San Francisco.

Thus it goes. People all over our broad land, and in other lands, want to have among them a representation of the face and figure of that man who was a friend of all the people and of whom Edwin Markham wrote:

THE LINCOLN STATUE, LINCOLN MEMORIAL, WASHINGTON, D. C.
DANIEL CHESTER FRENCH, SCULPTOR
By Courtesy of Georgia Marble Co.

The color of the ground was in him, the red earth;
The smell and smack of elemental things;
The rectitude and patience of the cliff;
The good-will of the rain that loves all leaves;
The friendly welcome of the wayside well;
The courage of the bird that dares the sea;
The gladness of the wind that shakes the corn;
The mercy of the snow that hides all scars;
The secrecy of streams that make their way
Beneath the mountain to the rifted rock;
That gives as freely to the shrinking flower
As to the great oak flaring to the wind,
To the grave's low hill as to the Matterhorn
That shoulders out the sky.

THE END